Praise for *Investing With Purpose*:

"This book has great value for all earlier stage entrepreneurs, and Mark shares his personal growth skills for everyone's benefit."

—Lee O'neill,
Executive Director of Urbana-Champaign
Angel Network, former President and
CEO of Busey Bank

"*Investing With Purpose* is an exceptional book! In a highly engaging manner, Mark Aardsma provides practical and proven approaches to investing in the creation of a fulfilling life. This is a book that every entrepreneur should read."

—Edgar Papke,
Leadership Coach and author,
The Elephant in the Boardroom

"I found myself desperately wishing I had read this book when I was 28. And yet now at the age of 58, being challenged that it is not too late to make some significant life changes regarding the resources in my life. Mark has done a masterful job of intertwining life experience and illustrations with principles demonstrating how to identify and make decisions regarding your resources, enabling you to live life to the maximum and positively impact your world."

—Dave Clark,
Christian Community Development Association,
Operations and Program Director

D0907650

CAPITALIZE ON THE TIME AND MONEY YOU HAVE
TO CREATE THE TOMORROW YOU DESIRE

INVESTING
With
PURPOSE

><

By

Mark Aardsma

THE CAREER PRESS, INC.
Wayne, NJ

INVESTING WITH PURPOSE
EDITED BY JODI BRANDON
TYPESET BY EILEEN MUNSON
Cover design by Rob Johnson/Toprotype
Cover Image by Bruce Rolff/shutterstock
Interior illustrations by Ian Riley
Printed in the U.S.A.

To order this title, please call toll-free 1-800-CAREER-1 (NJ and Canada: 201-848-0310) to order using VISA or MasterCard, or for further information on books from Career Press.

CAREER
PRESS

The Career Press, Inc.
12 Parish Drive
Wayne, NJ 07470
www.careerpress.com

Library of Congress Cataloging-in-Publication Data

CIP Data Available Upon Request.

TO ALL WHO ASPIRE

Acknowledgments

To you: Thank you for aspiring with me to invest well for the greater good.

To my wife, Jenn: Thank you for supporting the creation of this book with your quiet and active love.

To my friends Adam, Tim, and Tony: Thank you for batting around ideas and encouraging me in this project.

To my cousin Feather: Thank you for company and support in the writing sessions.

To fellow entrepreneur Cameron: Thank you for the music that became the soundtrack to my writing.

To my mentor Greg: Thank you for your steady belief in my greater potential.

To my mentor John: Thank you for working really hard on me with me.

To my mentor Edgar: Thank you for generously sharing your window on people and business with me.

To my former employee Phil: Thank you for inspiring the two best business ideas I've had so far, and for your companionship at the beginning of it all.

To my business managers Collin, Joey, Kim, Lynn, Mario, and Adrienne: Thank you for leading my companies to continued success.

To my assistant, Venus: Thank you for believing in this work and supporting me in the details.

To fellow entrepreneur Katie: Thank you for being among the first to show me the broad usefulness of my personal investing notes.

To entrepreneur and illustrator Ian: Thank you for seeing the value of this project, and for contributing your unique ability to communicate visually.

To my local editor, Susanna: Thank you for making my writing better, and for lending your personal presence to the process.

To my literary agent, Maryann: Thank you for your sharp insight, humble confidence, and strong advocacy.

To the print and audio publishing teams: Thank you for believing in this work and for investing your resources to produce it.

To my parents: Thank you for investing in me, and for teaching me initiative, resourcefulness, and grit. They have served me well.

Disclaimer

This book contains my best attempt to distill what worked and why from my experiences as an entrepreneur and an investor. Your results may vary. The advice in this book is not a substitute for professional tax, legal, or accounting advice.

Throughout this book I address the reader directly, and for simplicity and clarity I give recommendations in the form of imperative sentences. These should not be interpreted as specific instructions for any individual's situation. Portions of this book likely do not apply to your specific circumstances. Please exercise judgment before making investment decisions.

> Contents <

> Introduction <

What will you do with your potential? In this book, I want to invite you to clarify the future you aspire to, and equip you to make your aspirations reality by effectively investing the time and money you have.

You get to decide what you want. It might be to attain great wealth, to generously improve our world, or both. Maybe you want to build your organization into something much more than it is today. Perhaps lifelong learning and discovery are what you value most, or maybe it's living out your faith. You might aspire to triumph over what scares you, or to forge the fulfilling relationships you long for.

No matter what you aspire to, how you use the time and money you have will determine whether you make that future reality, or whether it will exist only as an unfulfilled dream.

At age 24 I was laid off, with just a few thousand dollars in savings. Instead of looking for a new job, I sat down at a makeshift desk in my basement and began to invest my time and money differently. Over the next 10 years I multiplied that savings a thousand-fold into a multi-million-dollar portfolio of businesses and other investments. During that time I also invested in my personal growth, transforming from a timid technician to a confident and capable CEO.

Along the way I created and refined a document that became my personal guidebook of time-and-money investment principles. When I grasped a new insight, or made a big mistake, I updated that document. When I felt afraid or confused about an investment decision, I reviewed that document to clarify my course.

This book is that guidebook in expanded form, illustrated with stories from my learning experiences. The investment rules in this book aren't about stock markets or financial wizardry. They are about how to use your resources effectively to get where you want to go. They work just as well today as they did thousands of years ago, before stock markets and even money were invented.

If you intentionally invest for a long time toward a deliberate future, you'll probably have more resources and more influence than most of the people you walk this earth with. Invest well.

Mark Aardsma

mark@aardsma.com

1 > Reflect Before You Race

Ten years before I wrote this, my employer lost the majority of its funding and I lost my job. I had a wife and two young children. We were partway through major renovations on the 104-year-old farmhouse we lived in, near a tiny town in rural Illinois. I didn't have a college degree, family with money, or an employment backup plan. We had recently spent most of our savings on materials for our home renovations. We had two or three thousand dollars to our name.

I didn't have enough money to invest, but I still got to be an investor. I got to decide how to use the resources I had, including my time.

The first investment decision I made was to become self-employed. Instead of hitting the streets to look for a new job, I stepped down the wooden stairs to the basement of that old farmhouse. I ducked under a beam at the bottom of the stairs, swept cobwebs away from my face, and looked around. It was creepy. The walls were old cinder block that someone had since sprayed with a green coating to keep water from seeping in. There were still plenty of slimy drip trails on the walls, with green algae that almost matched the coating. And it was cold.

I used one side of the old coal bin for one wall of my new office. A kitchen table from the 1950s became my desk. I moved my computer from upstairs, and connected it to my dial-up Internet modem. I wired a light fixture overhead, plugged in a space heater, and hung plastic drop cloths around three sides of the space to keep the warm air close. Total budget for my new office: $0 up-front and $0 a month.

Believe me, my first day sitting down at that desk was not filled with feelings of pride and self-assurance. I didn't even tell my friends what I was doing. I didn't want the embarrassment of explaining that it didn't work out.

I knew I wanted to support my family, stay productive, and build interesting things. I knew I was long on time and short on cash. I knew the highest-paying skill I had developed up to that time was computer programming. That day I searched the Internet for postings from small business owners offering to pay for custom software development. I actually did a small project for one of them and earned $59. I'd written software as a job before and made more than $59 in a day, but this was different. For the first time I owned the long-term value of the client relationship—and, much more importantly, I owned the copyright to the software I created. I wasn't just trading my time for cash to pay my bills for another day. I was building long-term value into something I owned. This incredible privilege of owning what I was building came to me courtesy of capitalism, and my willingness to take an emotional risk. That's it. It didn't cost me any money.

I had no idea, nor even a wish, that what I started building would lead to dramatic personal change and multi-million-dollar financial results. I did have just enough clarity about my bigger picture to guide the investment decisions I made that day.

Bring the Future Into Focus

At its core, investing is the practice of choosing your present actions intentionally to produce the results you want at a later time.

This is unnatural. We humans tend to reach for what we want now, and we find it difficult to look ahead to a later time. The present, with all its sensory experience, feels much more real than the future, which can only be imagined. We are not naturally investors. We are wired to prioritize short-term survival, not to maximize long-term results.

Sound investment thinking has totally different DNA. It's always looking ahead. It habitually imagines the future while making present decisions. It's always acting like the future is just as real as the present, because it is.

How are you at looking ahead? Try it with this scene.

A nurse, the smiling one in daisy-printed scrubs, guides your wheelchair down the hall, through the TV lounge, and outside the double doors. It's a warm day, perfect for sitting on the long, shaded, wooden porch.

She parks you at the far end and leaves you to the quiet afternoon. You're turning 100 tomorrow.

Wind chimes and sparrows provide background sounds as you reflect on a century of being alive. You worked hard. You met so many people—most forgotten, some that still make you wince a little, and some whose faces are bright and clear among the crowd.

Whom do you hope will be here tomorrow for your birthday party? You're told there will be a speech by your oldest friend. As you stare out across the lawn, you wonder what she'll say about you. How will she summarize a life of nearly infinite moments, decisions, and words? Accomplishments? Regrets? What do you hope she leaves out?

If you had a pen and paper handy, you could write some highlights for her. Tell her some things you *don't* want left out of your story. Maybe you'll just write the entire speech out for her, to make sure the story of your life is told the way you want it to be. Alas, you've nothing to write with, and your story has already unfolded in a million scenes.

You have the choice to live every day of your life as though you are writing that speech. You get to choose every action you take and every word you speak between now and the end of your life. Think bravely about what you want that speech to say, and live with purpose every day so that speech will be true. Intentionally author your legacy.

All your time taken together makes up your life. During your life you'll make a lot of choices about what to trade your time and your money for. Authoring your legacy on purpose is intentionally investing your time and money, on a whole-life scale.

Connect Each Piece to the Bigger Picture

You have the opportunity to act intentionally on the grand scale of your whole life, and at every smaller scale. With each smaller piece— perhaps a project, a relationship, or a hundred dollars—you can consider the outcome first. Intentionally choose the actions that are most likely to produce the outcome you want for that piece, and for that piece's part in the bigger picture.

Pieces come in all types and sizes. Here are some examples. Each list starts with a small piece and progresses through the bigger pieces it is part of.

Question	Stock Purchase	Sink Installation
⇩	⇩	⇩
Conversation	Stock Portfolio	Bathroom Remodel
⇩	⇩	⇩
Relationship	Investment Portfolio	House Remodel
⇩	⇩	⇩
Friendships	Saving for College	House Purchase and Sale
⇩	⇩	⇩
Social Life	Sources and Uses of Money	Real Estate Business
⇩	⇩	⇩
Impact on Others	Life Legacy	New Porsche
⇩		⇩
Life Legacy		Sources and Uses of Money
		⇩
		Life Legacy

And three more:

Question	Homework Assignment	Quiet Walk
⇩	⇩	⇩
Conversation	Final Exam	Day Off
⇩	⇩	⇩
Client Relationship	Class Grade	Stress Management
⇩	⇩	⇩
Sale	Semester GPA	Emotional Health
⇩	⇩	⇩
Sales Quota	Teaching Degree	Self-Care
⇩	⇩	⇩
Annual Bonus	Learning and Equipping	Personal Growth
⇩	⇩	⇩
Sales Career	Teaching Career	Mentoring Role
⇩	⇩	⇩
Charitable Project	Impact on Others	Impact on Others
⇩	⇩	⇩
Sources and Uses of Money	Life Legacy	Life Legacy
⇩		
Life Legacy		

How you stack your own cascades of intentions is a highly individual thing, based on what you value most. You might invest your money to achieve early retirement, whereas your neighbor invests hers to realize a dream of self-employment. You might build a relationship at work to ease your loneliness, while your co-worker builds a relationship at work to seek a promotion. The best decision for each piece is the one that's most likely to line up with what you want for the bigger picture.

"What you want" need not suggest selfishness, using people, or anything else that conflicts with your values. Your values and ethics are part of what you want, too. Hurting someone to get what you want isn't what you want if you value respect and generosity. Perhaps you want to live out your faith, give more than you receive, or put others ahead of yourself. If so, acting on purpose for the results you want will not conflict with those things because those things themselves *are* the results you want. Choose your present actions to bring about those things you truly want. Build what you value most into your bigger picture.

A few years ago I was visiting Ethiopia. I was there to learn about what creates and alleviates poverty. During my visit I was invited to meet with the staff and leadership of a nonprofit school. It was a hot and dusty summer afternoon, and classes had just let out for the day. Our hosts shared little cups of syrupy-sweet, charcoal-roasted espresso with us, and we all sat down to have a conversation. They had asked me to talk with them about planning and strategy.

I felt we needed to have a shared understanding of the school's reason for being before we could have a meaningful conversation about plans and strategy. The bigger picture would give us a light to hold the pieces up to and see where they fit.

Well aware that I was a newcomer and an outsider, I was in no position to share my opinion, or even have one. So I started asking questions. "What do you do here at the school?"

Most of the teachers were shy. One brave young woman said the obvious, "We teach children reading, math, music...?"

"What motivates you to get up every day and walk to work in the hot sun to do this?"

"We want the students to do well," they told me. "We want them to pass their exams and qualify for high school and college." They still seemed nervous about giving the wrong answer.

"And what motivates you to work hard at helping those students do well? Why?"

It was quiet in the room. Nobody answered for a minute. Then the principal of the school, an older man, said quite softly, "For a better Ethiopia." And that was it. I saw a deep love of country on the face of every person there. That was their bigger picture. "A better Ethiopia" was the legacy they wanted to leave.

That set the stage for a wonderful conversation about planning and deciding at the piece level, so the pieces might someday add up to that bigger picture they believed in.

Begin your foundation for sound investing with clear intentionality from the biggest to the smallest scale. It is impossible to define the ideal outcome of any single piece, even a financial investment, apart from the bigger picture of what you want. In order to be consistently intentional, you must connect the pieces into your bigger picture.

When I coach an entrepreneur on a business he or she wants to launch, I usually start with questions about the bigger picture: What's your ideal outcome from this business? Do you want to work here for a long time? Do you want to build it and sell it? How does this business fit into what you want your life to be like? The answers to questions like these influence decisions about corporate structure, financing, hiring, marketing—all of it. Every piece connects to the bigger purpose for the business, which connects to the bigger purposes of the entrepreneur's life. Going forward with those purposes disconnected or misaligned is a recipe for misery later on.

The day before I wrote this section I decided how to invest some money. This cash was sitting in a bank account earning nothing. I could have left it safely there, but I didn't. I didn't need that cash in reserve. I knew I wanted to earn more than zero on it because I always want to use all my resources as productively as I can. Why? One of my big intentions for my life is to leave this world a little better than I found it. Investing my resources productively so they grow helps me fulfill that intention. I had other, more immediate objectives, too. I knew that my plan was to do a business acquisition soon, and I'd need that cash then. My ideal outcome was to invest that money in something that would likely earn a good return and allow me to take that money back out in a few months. I bought a combination of stocks and bonds that fit the criteria that came from using my bigger picture as a guide.

Wait—the Bigger Picture Is Unclear

Maybe it's hard to describe what you want for a given piece of your life, work, or investments. It's probably harder still to connect it to what you want for each bigger piece above it. Maybe that chain from little piece to big legacy gets foggy somewhere in the middle. When you begin to organize the pieces into a bigger picture you'll find conflicts and contradictions between what you want for each piece. At best, parts of your bigger picture will be unclear and uncertain. That's life without a crystal ball.

It's not easy to reach clarity and alignment about your bigger picture. Nobody can hand you a personal values statement and life plotline summary. You have to figure them out in a process over time. Improving the clarity of your bigger picture is a lifelong pursuit.

There are two pitfalls here. One is winging it without taking time to reflect on the bigger picture. This leads to false starts, backtracking, and wasted resources. The other is getting stuck waiting for perfect clarity you'll never get. This leads to stagnation and wasted time. Fortunately, there is middle ground between perfect clarity from here to forever, and wandering aimlessly in confusion.

We know more than nothing and less than everything about our bigger pictures. Inability to see all the way to the horizon is no reason to fly with your eyes closed. Take time to reflect and bring your bigger picture into view as best you can. You will make far better decisions this way than if you wing it with no map at all, and you'll get far better results than if you sit and wait too long.

Many of the distant foggy parts clear up as you engage, take action, and move forward. With your best rendition of your bigger picture in mind, make the decisions that you deem most likely to lead to the results you want.

Effective investors make intentional decisions while at the same time dealing with uncertainty.

Watch Out When You've Lost the Bigger Picture

When you aren't guided by your vision for the bigger picture, you'll be vulnerable to undesirable influences on your investment decisions.

You might be tempted to default to the opinions of others. Don't lean on a stock tip, an opinion article, or the advice of someone who may not know what your investment goals are. You need a clear intention for the outcome to check recommendations from others against.

You might find yourself going along with what others want you to do: your family's vision for your career, the mutual fund your investment advisor wants to sell, or the business decisions that feel safest to the people closest to you. Some people have your best interests at heart, and some don't. Either way, it's a big mistake to default to someone else's game plan because your own vision is foggy. Your job as an investor is to decide. Don't abdicate your role as an investor by letting someone else make your decisions for you.

Imitating the crowd is another dangerous default behavior. All the people buying stocks during 1999's bubble couldn't be wrong, could they? Yes. Crowds do irrational things when it comes to investing time and money. If you follow the crowd you'll get average results, at best. You need your own compass that's not swayed by what everyone else is doing.

Doing what feels easy, familiar, or safe is a constant temptation. Your brain is wired with a strong priority to keep you alive. Sometimes the best investment decision, the one that fits your bigger picture, feels risky. Your brain doesn't realize that failed investments aren't life-threatening. Pay attention to your emotions and understand what they are signaling, but don't choose something just because it feels safe. You need a clear plan based on your bigger picture to guide your decisions more purposefully than your emotions alone can.

Clarity about what you want also provides motivation and resolve to do scary things, unpopular things, tiring things, boring things. Clear future vision helps you do things that don't feel good or easy or comfortable at the time.

Think Beyond the Obvious Answers to What You Want

Maybe we don't have to look far to know what we want. This is a book on investment. Don't we all simply want more money? Inside of almost all of us, it's deeper than that. Before we jump into strategy and tactics, here are some thoughts on money as a goal,

For the first part of my life I was relatively poor, then I had a middle-class income, and in recent years I've experienced an unusual level of wealth. Money is a wonderfully flexible resource. I've found wealth to be useful and worthy of attaining. The flexibility it gives me in what I trade my time for is precious to me. Having wealth also increases my opportunities to keep learning, inventing, and taking risks on new things. And it enables me to pay forward the kindnesses and generosities I've received in ways I couldn't do otherwise.

Some of the people I grew up around view wealthy people with suspicion and judgment. My sense after experiencing a wide range of income levels is that fear and envy, not realistic insight, were the source of those views. I have not found their views to match the reality of my experience.

Wealth is a powerful lever. Like a long crowbar, it can be used to do more than the strength of one person could otherwise do. If a wealthy person is authoring a legacy of hurting others, their wealth is a lever that can help them do more of that. If a wealthy person is authoring a legacy of generosity, innovation, or defending the vulnerable, their wealth is a lever that can help them do more of that. Wealth can be used to accomplish an astonishingly wide range of things, from destruction to building, from indulgence to philanthropy, from collecting stuff to enabling relational experiences. I want to make differences that matter while I'm alive. Some differences are hard to m......, want the most powerful levers I can get.

Like power or beauty, intelligence or strength, wealth can be used to help or to hurt. That doesn't make any of those things bad, it just makes them potent. Use all of them responsibly.

There's another part to this. Sometimes we use money to keep score of something else. Perhaps the score indicates ability to achieve, or status relative to other people. Every human being wants to feel capable, important, and wanted. Sometimes we think we want money because we want one of those deeper things, and we think money will help us get it. The thing is, we humans are deeply social, and we get the deeper things we need from how people treat us. Having more money doesn't necessarily cause people to treat us the way we'd like.

Money is useful for many things, but not all. Spending money on things money can't buy is a bad investment.

My experience has been that the hopes and fears of being me, the joys and heartbreaks of my relationships, the warmth of being loved, the loneliness of being ignored, and the thrills and frustrations of pursuing goals have felt the same all the way through. Being me doesn't feel any better or worse just because I have a lot more money than I used to.

If you don't like what it feels like to be you, you might be best served by investments in relationships, emotional healing, and personal growth. They'll cost you time and money, but they are quite different pursuits from growing your wealth.

If you put the advice of this book into practice, you will likely have more money later on than you have now. When you have a lot of money, then what? What do you want to use money *for*? What do you want to move with that big lever?

There are many worthy answers to that question. I hope you reflect before you race, and choose well.

Action Points

This book began as notes in a document for my personal use. I referred to it to remind myself of my investment principles as I evaluated tough decisions. The table of contents of this book looks a lot like the outline of that original document. Each chapter will end with summary points that expand on the table of contents. You might want to include some of them in your own decision guide.

▶ Choose your actions intentionally to lead to a future result, all the way through to the legacy you want for your life.

▶ Define what you want for each piece by connecting it to what you want for the bigger picture.

▶ Use your best rendition of your bigger picture to guide your decisions, though it will always be imperfect and subject to change.

▶ Guard against deferring to others or playing it safe when you've lost perspective on your bigger picture.

▶ If you want to increase your wealth, start with clarity about what you want to use wealth *for,* and ensure those purposes are things money can help with.

Engage Online

Share your bigger purposes and see what others are sharing at *www. aardsma.com/investingbook.*

2 > Value All Your Resources

I was in India, visiting Kolkata to strengthen ties with my company's textile suppliers there. It was my first experience making that kind of trip. I was wide-eyed and thrilled to be discovering new people and new places so far from home.

I took a car from the airport to my hotel on an undersized, ridiculously crowded road. Bicycles, goats, transport trucks, wooden wagons, and everything in between shared the narrow winding strip of pavement. At first the frequent horn honking seemed uncomfortably rude, until I started to see that it was an essential safety feature. The honking was not chaotic; it was expected communication meant to warn slower travelers on two wheels or two feet that they were about to be passed. I began to understand why driving is a trained profession there, not for the faint of heart.

During my visit I spent one day with a local tour guide. He was officially trained in the history and monuments of the city. He wanted to show me the high points and the tourist attractions, what he knew, and what he was proud of. I had a different goal: to continue to learn about poverty around the world. I wanted to see the daily life of real citizens in the city. Because he couldn't resist showing me the high points, I obliged. We went from place to place in our air-conditioned car, learning the history of the city.

After a few monument visits and some more persuasive discussion, I prevailed, and we went off the main roads into the alleys and back streets of the city. We saw homeless people sleeping in formerly grand buildings from colonial days. We visited markets with stomach-threatening smells. We stepped into religious places and ceremonies I didn't understand. We saw skilled artisans working with ceramics in small shops down narrow alleys and corridors.

Perhaps my guide was starting to believe that I honestly did want to see the real city. After all that, he took me to a slum. It was a shantytown along and down the banks of an urban ravine. Much to my surprise, pockets of this shantytown looked decidedly *industrial*. There were large square bales of something, sorted by color, and stacked beside the road. I saw piles, tin-roofed sorting areas, and people of all ages doing work. My tour guide explained. The people of this slum are recyclers. They separate materials of value from the trash of the city, and sort, clean, and bale them for sale. That's how they survive.

This glimpse of a way of life in a slum might make you uneasy. It probably should. It raises a lot of questions worth thinking about, and feeling about.

Here's one thought I took away. I'll never forget the resourcefulness of those people. They used resources we might not even think of as resources to increase their return on investment of time.

The first time I visited New York City, I took a walk from my hotel near Times Square, all the way down to the financial district in lower Manhattan. I had been intrigued by the workings of financial markets for years, and I had participated in them as a financial investor. I wanted to stand in front of the iconic New York Stock Exchange, the symbolic center of it all. So I did. I stood there and looked at that familiar, pillar-adorned structure, and I felt grateful for access to a system that let me participate, though I had no status, position, or anyone's permission. I wasn't sure what else to do there, so I took a selfie with the Wall St.

sign, bought some Greek yogurt from a shop around the corner, and walked back to my hotel.

I'm pretty sure the residents of that slum in Kolkata didn't own any stocks, bonds, or real estate. They certainly weren't using any fancy hedge fund algorithms. I bet they never had a transaction processed at the New York Stock Exchange. They may not have had bank accounts to store money, or even much cash. We might easily conclude that they had no resources to invest, but we'd be wrong. They had resources, and they were making investment decisions with those resources. They had that land in and around the ravine. They had each other. They had other people's trash. They used those resources to increase the return on the investment of their time resource from near zero, to enough to survive.

When I talk about investing, I'm referring to something more fundamental than what happens inside the New York Stock Exchange. The Wall Street exchanges, and financial instruments like stocks and bonds, are mechanisms for investing. Investing itself, as a concept, as a *practice*, is much broader and more basic. Investing existed long before the invention of money. Investing is using resources, of all kinds, to get more of the results you want in the future.

Money is a human invention to make trading and investing resources easier and more efficient. Thanks to money, if I have extra apples, and want some oranges, I don't have to find someone who has extra oranges and wants apples. Money also transports more easily and stores better than apples and oranges. These features make money a convenient intermediate between one kind of resource and another. We've developed ways to trade money for almost anything, and this is a really useful feature of advanced society. Fundamentally, money is a claim on other people's resources.

Money is the most flexible resource, but it's not the only resource that matters. The only way to get money in the first place (unless someone gives it to you) is to make effective investment decisions with your other, non-monetary, resources. Time, skills, physical stuff—value all your resources and include them in your intentional investment decisions.

Take Stock of Your Owned Resources

A resource is anything that's useful to you or someone else. If you get to decide or influence what a useful thing is used *for,* that thing is part of *your* resources.

The most straightforward examples of your resources are things you own. If you own a car, it is part of your resources because you get to decide what it is used for. The cash in your wallet is part of your resources for the same reason.

We learn about this as toddlers when we try to grab other kids' toys. We call it property rights. Law enforcement in developed countries protects, with force if needed, your exclusive right to decide the use of the resources you own. If someone tries to take the cash from your wallet or the car from your driveway and use it the way they want to, they can be arrested, and forced to repay you. By the same token, the lack of protection for property rights is an enormous obstacle to successful investment in many developing countries.

You also own some things that wouldn't typically be listed on a credit application or a personal financial statement. You own your body, your mind, and everything you've learned in your life. You own your time, because you get to decide what to use it for. These are all basic human rights protected by things like constitutions, and they are highly useful resources.

The chart on page 31 shows some more examples of non-financial resources you might own.

(See a longer brainstorm-style list of non-financial, investable resources at *www.aardsma.com/investingbook.* You can suggest additions there, too.)

▶ Conversation skills.	▶ Hobby gear or supplies.
▶ Sales ability.	▶ Emotional Intelligence.
▶ Power tools.	▶ Experience with tragedy.
▶ Foreign language skills.	▶ Retirement account.
▶ Commercial driver's license.	▶ Works of art.
▶ Degree or certification.	▶ Computer.
▶ Technical skill.	▶ Spare bedroom.
▶ Land your house is on.	▶ Customer list.
▶ Next year's tax refund.	▶ Patent or copyright.
▶ Software application.	▶ Rental property.
▶ 20/20 vision.	▶ Wardrobe of clothes.
▶ Fashion sense.	▶ Stock options.
▶ Industry contacts.	▶ eBay account.
▶ Car or truck.	▶ Work process or system.
▶ Trustworthy reputation.	▶ Warehouse space.

Include Your Vast Shared Resources

At the time of this writing, I'm working on training for my private pilot's license. When I drive to the airport tomorrow I'll travel over millions of dollars in roads that I don't own, and I get to use. I'll walk through a multi-million-dollar airport terminal that I don't own, and I get to use. I'll drive in my car that was produced with billions of dollars of car-manufacturing equipment that I don't own, and I got to use, indirectly, to get a very nice car for much less than a billion dollars.

I'll taxi the airplane (that I don't own, and get to use) across millions of dollars of concrete taxiways, and take off on a beautiful 1.2 *million*-square-foot runway, that I don't own, and get to use. A flight instructor whom I don't own (obviously) will use his hundreds of hours of training to assist me. I'll also be assisted by a national system of radar antennas, control towers, security personnel, and air traffic controllers that costs about $16 billion per year to operate. My cost for using it is zero dollars more than if I don't use it. And I can use it as much as I want. I guess in some sense that makes me a $16-billionaire.

Shared resources are everywhere. A church's building, a city library, a mentor's insights, Google, Wikipedia—we all have access to countless shared resources.

Those last two shared resources are Internet resources. The Internet is a massive shared resource worthy of special mention. Corporations and governments spent billions of dollars creating the Internet by connecting the world over fiber optic cables. None of us own the Internet, and if you are reading this book, you almost certainly get to use it for very little cost to you. The Internet is a resource that makes things possible that simply wouldn't have worked before, including the businesses I've succeeded with. The Internet makes investments in your learning, communication, marketing, digital product delivery, and almost everything else, more efficient and more accessible than ever before.

For thousands of years before you and me, other people invested their time and resources in creating technological advancements and the shared resources of advanced civilization. We all get to use them, as a free inheritance from generations past. If you are alive and breathing in this abundant, modern world, you have access to trillions of dollars in shared resources at little or no cost to you. This is not an exaggeration. How will you put those vast resources to use to produce the results you want in the future?

A fashion entrepreneur and friend of a friend used the shared resources of social media to build his rugged clothing brand from nothing. He used the shared resources of many prior textile and apparel technology inventions to inform and enable his manufacturing process. The sewing machine was essential, for example, and cost my friend nothing in invention effort or patent licensing costs. He used the shared resource of UPS to ship his product to a dispersed customer base, something that wouldn't have worked 200 years ago. He used the Internet for all kinds of free information about how to manufacture and market his products. He used the shared resource of word-of-mouth advertising to spread the word, and on and on. The shared resources he tapped into to make his brand a success were vastly greater than the owned resources he invested.

Furthermore, most of what he invested wasn't money. His sense of taste, his energy and insight for marketing, and his time to get it all off the ground were perhaps his biggest investments. If he had included only his bank account when evaluating the resources he could use to start that business, he would have underestimated what he was working with by 99 percent or more.

The same is true for you. Whether you have a lot of cash on hand, or none at all, you have access to abundant investable resources, vastly greater than at any previous time in the history of humanity.

Call Out Fear for What it Is

With so many resources at our disposal, why do we sometimes think and act like we don't have what we need to make investments in our long term? We talk ourselves into doing nothing with the resources we have by telling ourselves we don't have enough yet, or we need different resources before we can start investing in the future we want.

Even if you don't have what you need to build the future you want, you have resources that you can start employing, exchanging, and investing to get the other resources you need.

We all have enough resources to start building our future today. It's fear, not lack, at work when we dissuade ourselves from taking the reins as active investors of our resources. Fear that we'll run out of survival essentials. Fear that we'll fail in front of family and friends. Fear that we won't get what we want after all, and the heartbreak of trying will be greater than the vague disappointment of lowering our expectations before we even begin. It's fear that says, "I don't have what I need to do that, so I can't start." Honestly, lack of resources has nothing to do with it.

My friend Will invests in financial markets from his home in Swiss farm country. He also does some work for area goat farmers. These goats have the strength and agility to jump over any fence the farmers could realistically build around their sprawling pastures. Not to worry, though: The farmers have a technique for keeping them in that doesn't require creating real limitations.

When the goats are young and full of energy, the farmers keep them in a small pen. These goats promptly commence their best attempts to jump out of the pen. Because the fence around this small pen is high, and the goats are still small, they can't do it. Eventually, they give up. They conclude they don't have what it takes to jump fences. Once they reach that conclusion, they never try again. The farmers can let them out into the big pastures, with much lower fences. When the goats grow big, they never forget that fences are insurmountable. After all, they tried it 1,000 times already. They spend the rest of their lives "trapped" by fences they could hop right over.

We act a lot like those goats. We learn to see ourselves as helpless. We believe we don't have what it takes to pursue what we really want. We keep thinking and acting that way, because it protects us from risk, failure, and disappointment. It also "protects" us from taking the actions that will lead to the results we want.

It takes courage to want what you might not get. It's scary to set your sights on a destination you may never reach. Investing in an uncertain future is risky, and it feels even riskier.

You have abundant resources. Acknowledge your fears, and decide how to use your resources to build your future. Start with what you have, and build it into more.

Actively Decide How to Use Your Resources

Investors are deciders. As an investor, you decide how your resources will be used to produce the results you want in the future. Your resources include your self, your time, everything you own, and the vast shared resources you have access to. With every resource, we choose, consciously or not, how it will be used.

When we don't make a conscious and intentional decision about how to use a resource, it doesn't go away, of course, or cease to be used. It may be in storage, or continue to be used the same way it was before. Our time, for example, will be used for something (or nothing) even if we don't consciously and intentionally decide what to do with it. It's much easier and more natural to make passive, default, habitual resource decisions than to make conscious, proactive, intentional decisions.

Whether intentionally or by default, when we choose how to use a resource, we are choosing from the following menu of options.

Consume: Trade a Resource for an Experience

When you consume a resource, you trade it for an experience, and do not receive another investable resource in return.

When I burn natural gas in my furnace to heat my house, the resource is consumed. I trade natural gas for the experience of being warm. I don't receive any resource in return. When I eat food, I trade it for the experience of enjoyable eating, or maybe the experience of staying alive. If I buy new clothes, I trade money for the experience of looking a certain way. If I throw something in the trash, I trade it for the experience of having less clutter around.

It's not the type of resource used that determines whether a trade is consumption or not. If you receive something investable in return, it's an exchange. If you don't, it's consumption. For a business, an advertising expense intended to be an exchange for new customers can become consumption if no new customers respond. The key question is "What will I receive in return?" If you give something investable in trade for nothing investable, it's consumption.

Too much consumption can seriously hurt your long-term future, but consumption isn't always bad. Consumption is a valid and sometimes-necessary resource decision. We'll look further at the tradeoff between consumption and investment in Chapter 4.

Exchange: Trade One Resource for Another

You can trade time at a job for money, and money at the grocery store for food. You can trade cash for stock in a company, and stock in a company for cash. You can trade time practicing for a new set of skills. You can trade time in conversation or a purchased gift for a stronger bond in a relationship. You can sell something online for cash. You can plant a tree for cleaner air. You can give to causes for a better world.

When you trade a resource for another resource that's worth more, you grow your resources. This is trading up. In a perfect world, you'd trade up with every trade you make. Reality is uncertain and execution is complex, but the principle is the same.

We all make countless resource trading decisions every day. Right now you are trading your time reading this book for a benefit you hope to receive. It never stops. The power of choice means you get to make those exchanges intentionally, with your future in mind.

Save: Store a Resource for Use at a Later Time

Very often the time when you obtain a resource does not match the best time to put it to use. As investors, we can decide to save and store a resource, for use at a later time.

None of the tools in my garage are being used at this moment, but their value remains. They are being stored for use at a later time. A building contractor might store leftover materials until another job comes up. A bakery might keep cookies and cakes in a display case until they sell. We store food in refrigerators, money in saving accounts, and product inventory in warehouses. We store information on hard drives and in books. We store knowledge and skills in our brains and bodies. Your trusted reputation is a resource stored in the minds and hearts of other people.

In central Illinois, where I live, every town has a grain elevator with tall silos for storing grain. We harvest grain once a year, but feed cattle and eat cornflakes year-round. Storage makes that possible and thereby increases the usefulness of the grain harvest.

Most investment activities require first storing up resources, then deploying them into the new investment. Many investments require a sizable chunk of resources up-front, such as buying a business, creating a product, earning a degree, or building a new relationship. You must store up money, skills, and life resources that allow free time, for example, in order to take on those investments.

An abundant base of stored resources enables you to think and act differently from someone who feels like they barely have enough resources to get by. When you have chosen to save and store resources, you gain confidence, and you open up a lot more options. You can pay in advance if it saves enough to make it worth it. You can make a loan and earn interest instead of paying interest. You can absorb the shock of an unexpected expense without derailing your plans. You can say yes to resource-intensive opportunities when they come along. You'll be searching for those opportunities, because you want to put your stored resources to good use.

Storage retains value while offering us flexibility about when we use a resource. This simple ability to produce or acquire a resource at one time and use it at another time greatly increases our investment options. This is what makes inventions like food preservation (refrigeration, pasteurization, vacuum packing) and money preservation (banks, investment regulations) and property preservation (security systems, insurance) so valuable. "Use it later" offers myriad more options than "use it now."

Employ: Use a Resource to Accomplish Something Without Using it Up

A hammer greatly reduces the investment of time required to drive a nail into a 2 × 4. Almost magically, after driving a nail, the hammer gave a valuable return in the form of freed-up time, yet became no less valuable in the process. The laptop I'm using to type this is being neither exchanged nor consumed in the process. A structural engineer's knowledge is neither exchanged nor consumed when he uses it to design a bridge.

Investing is trading a resource now for something that's worth more later. The hammer, the laptop, and the engineering knowledge cost less to obtain than the value they can provide over their lifetime. Resources like these, which give value without being used up, can be incredibly valuable long-term investments. This is one of the ways investment decisions grow your resources, almost magically turning a little into a lot more.

Many of our shared resources work this way, too. Wikipedia and the local library add value to our endeavors, and lose no value when we use them more. All kinds of tools, equipment, and information resources can be used to create value without losing their value. We have the choice to trade our time and cash for long-term employable resources like these.

My 13-year-old son earned money last winter shoveling snow for our neighbors. His goal is to purchase a new video game console. The entertainment experience he'll receive from that video game console is consumption. He will not receive an investable resource in return. He uses a shovel to clear those driveways of snow, and earns about $10 for an hour's hard work. The other day I suggested he consider delaying his video game consumption so he could trade some of the cash he is earning for a gas-powered snow blower. This investment in an employable snow blower resource would allow him to earn about $50 an hour instead of the $10 an hour he's making now. The huge increase in productivity would recover his investment in the snow blower within weeks, and provide enough income to purchase 10 video game consoles (or expand his yard care business) this year. As of this writing, he's still thinking about it.

Lend: Receive Compensation for Temporary Use of a Resource

When you save excess resources and store them, you can usually also lend them at the same time. You can lend extra money to your bank and receive interest as compensation. You can lend an extra house to tenants, and receive rent as compensation. You can lend money to a business by purchasing its stock. (The purchase of stock is both exchanging and lending. You exchange cash for a loan someone else already made.)

When a loan (in the broadest sense) is repaid at a fixed amount of money, we usually call it a loan or a bond. When it's repaid in a share of profits, we call it equity or stock. Either way you are giving up the use of your resource for a time, in exchange for compensation.

Of course, you'd expect to receive more back then you originally lent. Renting out your extra resources in one way or another is an important avenue to growing your resources.

Borrow: Give Compensation for Temporary Use of a Resource

Borrowing, of course, is the opposite of lending. When you pay for the use of someone else's stored resources, you are the borrower and they are the lender. They will expect to receive more back than you originally borrowed, making this an easy way to shrink your resources—unless you grow what you borrowed a lot before you return it. We'll talk more about debt and leverage in Chapter 12.

Action Points

▸ Use all your resources, not just financial instruments like stocks and bonds, to produce the results you want later.

▸ Use both the resources you own and the vast system of shared resources you don't need to own in order to use.

▸ Confront any fears that hold you back, and get started with the resources you have.

▸ Actively decide the use of each resource: consume, exchange, save, employ, lend, or borrow.

Engage Online

See a reader-contributed list of non-financial resources you might use to reach your goals, or add to it at *www.aardsma.com/investingbook*.

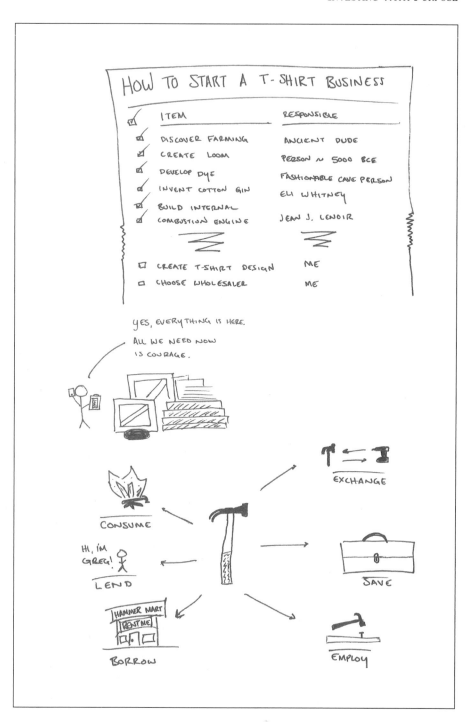

3 >   Tell Yourself the Truth About Time

A few months into my basement software freelancing, things were going just fine. I was earning a nice hourly wage, paying my bills, and saving some money. I wasn't working for an employer, and I was still trading my time for money. I was grateful for this success in generating the income I needed, and at the same time I was starting to feel uneasy. My workdays were full. I couldn't bill any more hours without working nights or weekends. I've never been a workaholic, and I wasn't about to become one to grow my business. Besides, what would happen when my nights and weekends became full? 24/7 is a hard-stop limit on time. Non-negotiable. I needed a different solution.

About that time I took a project to modify an e-commerce Website for a client. The modifications he wanted were small. I think I quoted him $120 to make the changes. He was using a large e-commerce software package to run his Website, and I wasn't familiar with it. As I dug into that software package I found it was undocumented, and complex. I spent an entire day of non-billable time learning how the system worked. It seemed like a pretty bad trade at the time. My effective hourly rate on that project was plummeting rapidly.

The next day I completed the modifications for the client. There I was with this newly acquired knowledge of the software package, and nothing else to do with it. I felt silly for spending so much time to figure it out. Hoping to redeem myself, I Googled to see if I could find other users of that software who might need work done on it. Within a few clicks I stumbled on an active forum where about 3,000 users of the software interacted. Some of them had the same problem I had just fixed for my client. All of them were looking for help.

In this I saw a new and different kind of investment opportunity. I began trading less of my time for an hourly wage, and instead traded that time to create software products of lasting value. I created installable modifications in the form of plugins that were useful to many of those 3,000 users. Those software products were resources that I owned, that could be used without being consumed. I was no longer limited by the number of hours in a day. I could sell as many copies as I could find buyers for, and I did.

Those investment decisions I made in my basement grew my resources faster than I ever expected. They still had nothing to do with stocks, bonds, or Wall Street. The resource I created when I studied that software package for a day wasn't visible, tangible, or monetary. Nonetheless, it was a resource I was able to trade for hundreds of thousands of dollars. The hard limit of 24 hours in a day was no longer a limit on what I could earn. I traded what I had, and my resources grew beyond what trading my time for an hourly wage could ever have accomplished.

Time: A Peculiar and Precious Resource

Time—that is, hours, days, and years being alive—is one of your resources. As an investor of all your resources, you get to make decisions about what you trade your time for. Investment principles apply to time just as well as physical stuff and financial resources. Time is like other resources in that we get to make investment decisions about what we trade it for. You can invest your time toward an intentional future. Time also has some special characteristics as a resource, and these peculiarities make your decisions about how you invest your time extremely important.

Time is special because it's given out to everyone at an equal rate, for free. You may not receive the same amount as another person, but you will receive it at the same pace. You get a fresh installment of 24 hours every day, as long as you are alive. Regardless of wealth, position, location, gender, race, or any other quality, time ticks at the same speed for all. It's like passing go and collecting $200 in Monopoly. You receive it automatically, even if you are at the very beginning of the game and not yet receiving a return from any investments. This means everyone alive always has a valuable resource to make investment decisions with. In life (unlike Monopoly) you can't go resource-bankrupt as long as you are alive. You always have time to trade for something else.

Time is special because it and our bodies are the only things we come into the world owning. Unless you are given a lot of resources early in life, time is the resource you use to prime the pump of investment. It's the resource you trade for most other resources you will own and invest. This means your decisions about how you invest time are hugely impactful, especially early in the process of growing your resources. Life is a grand exercise in starting with time and shared resources, and trading for everything else. The results of your trading might be deep relationships, generous impact, wealth, or all of the above. What you trade for is up to you.

Time is special because it can't be saved or stored. Just like every living person's pace of receiving time is constant and equal, every living person also uses time at the same constant pace that it's received. We use our time as it's given, whether we want to or not, whether or not we consciously decide what to use it for. This is a big limitation. Imagine having to decide every minute what to spend a dollar on, ready or not. Time works like that. We have to spend a minute, every minute, ready or not. Partially mitigating this extreme restriction, time can be traded for other resources that can be saved and stored, thus increasing our flexibility and investment options.

Time is special because it's strictly limited. Our bodies are remarkable in their ability to maintain themselves, heal, and last a long time. Your heart will likely beat more than 2 billion times in your lifetime, in the course of almost a million hours. As humans, we far exceed most other species at this business of living long. Nonetheless, time being alive on earth is a very limited resource. Some people get a lot less than 100 years; nobody gets much more. Many people will receive more dollars in life than they will receive hours. Some people will receive more dollars in life than they will receive heartbeats! From an individual perspective, most other resources are far less limited than time is.

Time is special because, though time can be traded for more of other things, other things cannot be traded for more time. (At least not much more. We might buy medicine that increases our odds of living a full lifespan, for example, but so far nothing extends the human lifespan much beyond 100 years.) Trading time is a one-way thing. Almost all other trades are reversible. Time trades aren't. If you trade an hour for $20 in wages, you can't turn around and trade $20 for an additional hour of lifespan. It is possible to trade resources such as money for the use of other people's time, thus freeing up your own. This is delegation, one of the most powerful trades you can make. Although delegation doesn't increase lifespan, it does open up possibilities for what you can do during your life. We will explore delegation in depth in Chapter 13.

Time is given freely, strictly limited, and un-storable. The hours of our lives can be spent, but more lifetime can't be purchased. These special qualities ought to lend a sense of gravity to our decisions about what we trade our time for.

A Tale of Two Workers

Two strong young men each agreed to summer work clearing land of brush and trees. They were tasked with clearing one acre apiece, and would be paid each day based on how much land they cleared. The first worker showed up early on the first day and worked hard. Using the axe, machete, and shovel provided by his employer, he cleared a small portion of his acre. Dirty, sweaty, and tired, he collected his pay for the day's progress. That evening he spent part of his earnings on good food and entertainment. Feeling quite satisfied, he went to bed on time, got some rest, and was back at it clearing land early the next morning. He did the same for two months of weekdays, until the work was complete. His was an admirable and profitable summer. He traded two months of his time for two months' fair wages. He supported himself honorably, enjoyed a pleasant lifestyle, and had some cash left over. Being a responsible planner, he even put some of that leftover cash in a retirement account, to save for a day when he wouldn't be an able-bodied worker anymore.

In a different part of the county, the second worker began just the same way. He showed up early on the first day and worked hard. Using the tools provided by his employer, he cleared a small portion of his acre. Dirty, sweaty, and equally tired, he collected his pay for the day's progress. That evening he spent his entire day's earnings on a used chain saw and a gallon of gasoline. He ate whatever was in his cupboards at home. Though he worked equally hard, he went to bed with less dinner and less cash in his pocket than the first worker. (It almost seemed unfair.) In effect, he traded a day of his time for a chainsaw and some gasoline.

The next day, chainsaw in hand, he showed up early and worked hard. He cleared twice as much land as the first day. Dirty, sweaty, and still quite tired, he collected his pay for progress, twice what he earned the day before. That evening, he spent all of his pay to rent a small tractor for one day. After another dinner of whatever was in his cupboards, and another night's sleep, he headed back to work. With the tractor and the chainsaw, he cleared the rest of the acre that day. Dirty, sweaty, and still quite tired, he collected the remaining pay for the entire acre, and returned the tractor. He traded three days of his time for two months' fair wages and a chainsaw. (It almost seemed unfair.) The next morning he inquired into the price of buying a tractor of his own.

After a few years of repeating similar investment decisions, our first worker would likely still have a responsible and respectable lifestyle. Our second worker would likely be wealthy and have a lot of free time if he wanted it. They both started with the same resources. This vastly different result flows from the difference in *what they traded their time for* early on. We all face similar choices.

Timing matters. If our first worker spent a few years trading his time for cash, and then decided to buy a chainsaw and a tractor, he would never catch up to the second worker, who made high-return trades with his investments at the beginning. The earlier you trade your time for resources that increase your return on investment, the better. This is because good time trades increase the return on investment of *all your remaining time* and they start the process of earning returns on not-your-time resources, like capital, equipment, or employees' time.

Trading your time to learn a marketable skill increases the trading value of your time for the rest of your life. Learning a marketable skill in your last year of life has a much different impact than learning the same skill several decades earlier. Investing financially is also highly time sensitive due to the exponential "snowball effect" of compounding. Starting to save and invest money a few years earlier makes a dramatic difference in the total result. Today is a better time to start than tomorrow.

Nothing affects our bigger future more dramatically than our time trade decisions. In spite of this, it's not natural to value our time and invest it wisely. Most people I am familiar with make investment choices much more like the first worker than the second worker. They trade their precious, limited time for survival and a lifestyle, and little more. With the right trades, and the right perspective on time, it's possible to achieve survival, a nice lifestyle, and a whole lot more.

Our Distorted Lens on Time

Multiple aspects of human nature conspire to distort our view of time, and our choices related to time trades.

Sensory experience is locked in the present. We are biased to put more weight on what we can see, touch, and otherwise experience than on what we can only imagine. This distorts our view of time. Out of sight tends to be out of mind, and the future is always out of sight. It takes faith, vision, and imagination to treat the future like it's real when we can't see it yet. This biases us to base our time trades on immediate circumstances and desires, to the detriment of our long-term circumstances and desires.

Backward beer that produced a hangover first and happy intoxication the next morning would no doubt be quite unpopular. Wise investment decisions are backward like that, too, and perhaps similarly unpopular.

Great investors keep the future in sight through their vision and imagination. They aren't overpowered by the sensory experience of the present. Their sense of the future is strong, so strong they can almost taste it. This visionary clarity is a huge investment advantage.

Another distortion in our view of time comes from the discomfort we feel when we are aware of our mortality. Pretending we will live forever feels better than planning for a real future that includes running out of time. It's unsettling. We don't like unsettling feelings, so we think and act as if they aren't real.

I think we go through life acting like we have more to lose than we really do, because we forget the ending. We are given our minds and bodies and a vast array of other resources to use, temporarily. Nothing we can do will make this arrangement other than temporary. If we remember this, I think we will focus more on using the time well. We'll become more proactive, more risk-taking, and less likely to hunker down in a small life partially comforted by the thin illusion that we can keep it.

Perhaps the most powerful distortion in our lens on time comes from how strongly we are wired to survive. Our biology vigilantly prioritizes survival over all else, and it has a point. If we don't survive, we forfeit all our remaining time. A rabbit running for its life from a predator would not be well served to stop and gather supplies for winter. Survival must be the top priority when survival is threatened. Our long-term plans might be all for naught if we aren't alive to carry them out.

I think our brains take this survival priority too far. They aren't good at telling the difference between bona fide threats to our survival, and scary things that really can't hurt us. They take a "better safe than sorry" approach, and panic equally in all risky scenarios. The parts of our brains that control fear and prioritize survival are powerful. They don't understand time, don't do math, and don't do long-term scenario planning. They just keep us alive, today.

In the safe, wealthy, and abundant societies a lot of us live in, we have time and resources for more than running from predators. Our survival is not at all threatened during our regular daily existence. Our brains haven't quite caught up to that reality.

Our low-level fear brains don't give reliable guidance when it comes to risks and rewards of participating in capitalism, and investment decisions in general. For example, embarrassment and lost money are not actually fatal, but we often act like they will be.

In response to these signals from our fear-prone brains, we tend to choose things that feel safe now, and let survival take priority over an optimal future. That's probably the best decision-making priority for a rabbit living on a prairie frequented by predators. If you are reading this book, you almost certainly have the luxury of a much more secure existence than that prairie rabbit. In spite of the reality that starvation and being eaten by predators are not significant risks for most of us, we still tend to act like scared rabbits. Our instincts scream "survive today; let the future take care of it itself." It's in our DNA, but as humans in prosperous societies, it's far from the best way to decide how to use our resources.

A Ugandan friend of mine leads a charitable organization that helps farmers in Uganda produce more crops and get them to markets more efficiently. I talked with him from time to time and heard updates on their progress as a new charity. Distribution of superior corn seed and education on farming methods were successful, and the crop was looking good. The amount of corn produced was twice what the same farmers had grown on the same land the season before. We were excited about how these farmers would benefit.

The time came to harvest the crops, and the harvest was a success. The employees of the organization rented a truck to transport the crops from the remote rural area to markets in the city. This transportation to market was a key link in the chain, allowing much higher sales prices for the crops. The rural farmers did not have the resources to accomplish this transportation to market on their own.

When the truck arrived at the farms, they found no crops there to pick up! My friend was dismayed to learn that the farmers had already sold the crops from their big harvest. A local crop trader had offered them half price to buy the crops now, rather than waiting a week or two for the truck to arrive, take the crops to market, sell them, and *then* pay the farmers. The farmers accepted that offer, and sold the crops for half price, giving up all the benefit they would have gained from the higher yields that season.

We may dismiss the investment decisions those farmers made as obviously foolish, and in some ways it was. Remember, though, that those farmers have legitimate reason to worry about physical survival more than you probably do. What if the crops never made it to market, or the money from selling them never made it back? What if the crops were stolen before the truck arrived? What if the nonprofit organization couldn't be trusted? Their families might face starvation. Selling for half price, cash in hand right now, ensured their family's survival for another season. Sending those crops to market for full price didn't.

Their circumstances, and their mindset, suggested prioritizing short-term survival over maximum long-term results.

We are hard-wired this way. We may fancy ourselves smarter than those farmers, but the truth is we are subject to the same distortions. We often make decisions that are very much like their choice to sell their crop for half price. Our obsession with survival distorts our view of the future.

When we look at time through a distorted lens, we don't take actions that create the future we want. We act based on today, and perhaps tell ourselves that we will get to building the future we want later. In the meantime we miss our most valuable opportunities to make those early time trades and investments that start the compounding process. We trade our time for too little, and we consume what we trade it for too readily. We spend our time on the safe, obvious, expected, and routine, rather than trading it for what we want most in our futures. We don't take enough risk in the present. We wait too long to confront our conflicts, get out of unproductive situations, and make big changes. We think we have time to kick the can down the road. And it costs us way more than half the price of those crops.

When we tell ourselves the truth about time, we give ourselves a chance to make very different choices—choices that will lead to the future we want.

Action Points

▸ Don't unknowingly trade a lifetime for a lifestyle by trading time for money and consuming it all.

▸ Treat your time like a treasure that's more rare and valuable than abundant resources like money and property.

▸ Trade your precious, limited time intentionally toward the future you want.

▶ Trade for resources that increase the productivity of your time, especially early in life.

▶ Watch out for natural distortions in your view of time, and the bad investment decisions that flow from those distortions.

▶ Make investment decisions as if the future is just as real as the present, because it is.

Engage Online

See how other readers reacted, and share your thoughts on our precious, limited time at *www.aardsma.com/investingbook*.

4 > Stick With the Folding Tables

After a year and a half in my basement, it was time to move my software business to an office. Though it would cost more, it would protect the privacy of my wife and kids, and create a healthy separation between work life and home life.

We lived in the country, near Piper City, a small town of just 800 people, a grain elevator, and a main street business district that's just one block long. Decades ago those main street buildings housed a bank, a car dealership, a barbershop, a furniture store, and more. Some of the residents and leaders of the town didn't want to admit it, but most of that was long gone and wasn't coming back. Some of the buildings were vacant, some were in use, but none were in their prime.

I called the mayor and asked him if he knew of some office space available to rent. He put me in touch with a couple of building owners, and I worked out a deal with one of them to rent the front half of 15 W. Main St. It was one big room of about 2,500 square feet. It had been a construction office, a small engine repair shop, a pool hall, a dress shop, a furniture store, and probably some other things. Now it was about to become a software office. I and my employee had two 6-foot folding tables, our computers, and our office chairs. We set those up by the front door, and we were moved in. Our setup took up less than one-twelfth of the space we had rented.

Ten years later, I own that building, and three others on the same side of Main Street. At my companies, we aren't in the software business anymore, but dozens of employees work there, doing 5,000 percent more business than we were doing when we moved in. A few years ago we converted the second story of 15 W. Main from a dusty attic, untouched for generations, to an additional floor of offices for our growing staff. One of those offices is mine, and in it stands one of those original folding tables. It's still my desk.

Those expansions of our office space were productive investments in future business returns. They weren't risky speculation. We had the sales and earnings growth to prove we'd need the space and make a profit on it.

Having more office space increased future returns, but upgrading my office furniture wouldn't have. Can I afford new office furniture? Sure. I haven't upgraded from the folding table because that would be consumption, not investment. I see neither emotional nor financial return from upgrading. Those businesses are Internet based. I don't meet clients in that office. I have no visitors whom I need to impress. New office furniture wouldn't do a thing to improve sales or earnings of those businesses, and it wouldn't do a thing to improve my workday experience. I'm serious about evaluating the return on my resource-use decisions. I'm sticking with the folding tables.

See Consumption and Investment in Contrasting Colors

Consumption is trading resources for anything that doesn't contribute to a future increase in your resources. Consumption may provide an immediate benefit, and that benefit comes at the cost of immediately and permanently reducing your resources.

Investment is trading part of your resources for something that does contribute to a future increase in your resources. It's trading for something that, over time, is worth more than what it cost you. Something that provides a return.

Both consumption and investing use resources in the present. They each lead to very different results in the future. To be an effective investor of all your resources, you must not mix consumption and investment into a vague gray of "spending resources." You must see them as polar opposites, like vividly contrasting colors.

Conrad and Ivanna are highly fictional characters stranded on a small, otherwise-uninhabited island.

They each have 24 hours of time per day to use as they choose. Drinkable water and adequate shelter are naturally available. They each need to eat five fish per day to survive for long. They want to use their resources to develop a way to get back to civilization and reunite with their families.

With immediate survival top of mind, they quickly discover how to catch fish by hand in the shallow water surrounding the island. It's frustrating, it's time-consuming, and it works. The first day they each catch five fish between sunup and sundown. They eat them raw, and retreat exhausted and sunburned to their shelter for the night.

As the sun rises the next morning, they wade out into the shallows to catch their meals. Again they each catch five fish, eat them raw, and sleep another night.

The next morning, Ivanna is bothered by the realization they are not getting ahead. They are spending all their time to produce resources and consuming them just to survive. As Conrad wades out to fish, Ivanna decides to use her time differently that day. With stomach growling she climbs up a hill to overlook the island and notes resources at hand. There are bushes, trees, rocks, a stream, sand, birds, and various grassy plants.

She gathers some thin branches and grassy reeds in a pile on a flat rock at the top of the island. She sits down and begins to braid the grasses into thin ropes. As she works she feels the discomfort of hunger, and sees Conrad on the beach below, eating a fish he just caught.

He wades out to try to catch another, and she continues to use her time to braid dozens of long thin ropes.

As Conrad goes to sleep that night, Ivanna continues working by moonlight. As the sun rises he awakes to find her sleeping, with dozens of fish piled nearby. Amazed at her late-night fishing success, he wakes her to ask the source of this good fortune. He learns, as you have surely guessed, that she has built a fishing net. She can haul in 10 fish with about an hour's work.

She limited her consumption and *invested* her time and a few natural resources in something that *increases productivity.*

That day they reach an agreement: Ivanna will rent Conrad her fishing net for a price of five fish per day, all she needs to survive. Conrad will fish one hour per day and catch 10 fish, enough to pay the rental fee and provide for his own survival.

Two days ago Ivanna had to work her entire day just to eat enough to survive. From now on she doesn't have to spend any time at all on food for survival. Why? Because she limited her consumption, created a surplus of time for a day, and invested it to create something that pays back far more than it cost, day after day, for a long time.

What's more, her investment in productivity was not at Conrad's expense. If he was fishing 12 hours a day before, his agreement with Ivanna frees 11 hours of his time per day as well. Investment in productivity is not a zero-sum game.

Consumption and Investment Compete for the Same Resources

In their simple scenario, our castaways could use their time resource to get enough food for a day's consumption, or they could invest their time resource in something of lasting value. Whatever time they spent fishing wasn't available to invest, and whatever time they spent building nets wasn't available for fishing.

The same is true for us in the real world. Real life contains a larger number of opportunities and greater complexity, but the principle is the same. Money spent on rent is no longer available to buy stocks or start a business. Two hours spent enjoying entertainment can't also be spent creating a new product.

You get to decide how to divide your resources between consumption and investment. Take a vacation, or new equipment for your business? Bigger house payment, or bigger contribution to your retirement account?

Housing and transportation are the biggest consumption expenditures of American households (source: *www.bls.gov/news.release/cesan. nr0.htm*). The kind of house you live in and the kind of car you drive are likely a big portion of your total consumption. Consume too much of your resources on big items like these, and your investing hands will be tied. Frugality on the little things (skipping Starbucks, or cheaper office supplies) can't overcome the headwinds of over-consuming on the big things (a big mortgage, or undisciplined labor costs).

Trading your time to simply consume more than you need to survive is a very expensive decision, especially early in life and when your resources are few. Most people in developed countries make this decision continuously throughout their lives. If you spend all your working life at a job, and consume (rather than invest) the entire proceeds of that job, you will never start the virtuous cycle of investment. The end result of that approach will be far fewer resources, and even far less opportunity to consume than through the alternate approach of limiting consumption in order to save and invest.

Limiting Consumption to Increase Investment Leads to Abundance

When you choose to limit consumption, as Ivanna did, and direct those resources to investment activity instead, you start a positive spiral of increased productivity and growing resources. Investments pay returns, increasing total resources. If those additional resources are invested, and not consumed, those new investments pay still more returns. This is the positive spiral of compounding. The long-term effect is a dramatic increase in resources.

Ivanna's investment allowed much greater consumption in the future than if she had never been willing to be hungry for a little while. This happened quickly in our island story because the productivity gain from the fishing net was a huge 2,400 percent. Dramatic returns like this are possible in the real world too, but often investment returns are much lower. Even with a modest 10-percent gain from investing resources, savers still pull ahead of consumers over time.

Consider a frugal saver who limits her consumption to 70 percent of her total income, and invests the other 30 percent at a 10-percent after-tax annual return. (Stocks and bonds would likely return less than that. If she invested where she had an advantage, such as a certain business, her returns would likely be much more.) For the first 13 years she would consume less than a neighbor with the same income who consumed 100 percent of his income. Looking over the fence at her neighbor's superior lifestyle could make it hard to believe that her decision to consume less and invest more was a wise choice.

She would have the equivalent of four years' income in savings at 13 years; maybe that would be some consolation.

For all years following, she would be consuming more than her non-saving neighbor, and still investing 30 percent of her total income each year. Fifty years after beginning this program, she would be able to consume three times what her neighbor was consuming each year, and she'd have *34 years' worth of income* in savings. He'd have none. By this time the benefits of her early-years choice to limit her consumption would be obvious. If around the time it became obvious, her neighbor started looking over the fence and wondering about his 100-percent-consumption choice, it would be too late for him ever to catch up to his frugal neighbor.

If our frugal saver limited her consumption to 50 percent of her income, and invested the other 50 percent, her consumption would catch up to her non-saving neighbor in just nine years. See the link at the end of this chapter to download a spreadsheet and experiment with the actual numbers from this example.

One of the most powerful things you can do for your financial future is consume less in the present, and invest more for the long term. This willingness to limit present consumption in order to produce a large investable surplus makes the difference between a lifetime of treading water, and a future of growing resources.

At the time of this writing (2015), the average American spends 95 percent of their income on consumption, leaving just 5% for investment (source: *https://research.stlouisfed.org/fred2/data/PSAVERT.txt*). If you choose to limit present consumption in order to save and invest a much higher percentage than that, you won't have to move the consumption setting many notches to come out far ahead of your American neighbors.

Survival Demands a Base Level of Consumption (and Cash)

Unfortunately, reality doesn't let enthusiastic savers take this concept of limiting consumption to the extreme. If you consume nothing, and invest 100 percent of your resources, you'll starve to death. If at any point you don't survive, the rest of your time—your most precious resource—will be forfeited.

Your survival requires air, water, food, shelter, mental health, and maybe some other things. Your first and permanent baseline task is to ensure your resources are sufficient to provide for your survival. Only when you have surplus resources (those resources not needed for your survival) can you decide to invest, or do anything other than survive.

In the beginning, you'll probably need to trade your time for resources, and consume them in order to survive. This means produce them directly, or work for money to get the water, food, and shelter you need to survive. In developing countries this might be subsistence farming or working for day wages. In developed economies this usually means having a job. A job consumes a great deal of time, and this usage of your most precious resource should not be taken lightly. The key is to limit your consumption and thereby create an investable surplus as soon as possible.

In business, cash is oxygen. Run out of it, and you'll be dead in short order. A bottle of oxygen won't help if it's an hour late, and extra cash next year won't help a business stay alive either. It's impossible to make decisions for your long term while gasping for air. When survival is in question, survival naturally and necessarily becomes top of mind. The only way to avoid this is to produce more than you consume, and save a surplus. It's much easier to think like an investor when you have extra cash on hand.

The same is true of personal life. Many households live paycheck to paycheck, and that situation forces decisions that produce short-term gain for long-term pain.

One of my business buildings sits next to a gas station. I've observed people who visit it multiple times per week, putting $5 of gas into their car at a time. My mind protests the time resource they spend driving there, filling up, paying, and driving off. I bet it amounts to 30 minutes a week for some people. Do that for a decade (as some do) and the total time cost is about 250 hours, equivalent to a month of full-time work. During that decade, I estimate our frequent-filler would also consume about *20 tanks* of gas on the mile or two back and forth to the gas station. If this person generates enough surplus cash to invest in completely filling the tank just *one time,* no additional investment will be required ever to enjoy the time and fuel savings of minimizing trips to the gas station.

If our frequent-filler currently spends $15 per week on gas, then decides to invest in a complete fill, he'll spend perhaps $50 that week on gas. For all weeks for the rest of time, his expense goes back to what it would have been ($15 not counting changes in gas prices).

This is an extreme example of making decisions to maximize immediate cash flow at the expense of long-term results. This is managing to cash flow instead of to maximum return. It's a vicious cycle. If you are in it, do whatever it takes to generate a surplus that frees you from that cycle. You only have to do it once, for a lifetime of benefit.

When we are managing to cash flow instead of long-term results, we do things like habitually pay interest on credit card balances, take lower-paying work because it pays sooner, or repair a worn-out machine repeatedly to avoid the big cash outlay of replacing it. These may not be as obviously shortsighted as frequent trips to the gas station, but the principle and the results are the same.

Because cash is oxygen, credit cards or other convenient sources of borrowing might seem like a handy way to keep breathing when income and bank accounts run low. The long-term cost of using credit in this way is invisible at first, but soon creates a hole that's expensive and difficult to climb out of. Except in emergencies, live within your means so you have extra cash in the present, and the freedom to do what's best for your long term, even if it reduces your cash up-front.

I do not lack compassion for the survival pressures that frequent-fillers, and their equivalents in others areas of life, are dealing with. I earnestly long to see them make different investment decisions and escape the cycle of managing to cash flow. If they work a couple hours of overtime, or forego enough consumption to create just one tank of surplus, so to speak, they can permanently improve their situation. (So far no gas station patrons have asked my opinion, and I have refrained from leaning out of my office window to offer unsolicited advice.)

Focusing on long-term returns without concern about short-term survival is a luxury that's available to many more people than are currently enjoying it. If you are an able person living in a country with a functioning economy, rule of law, and a few other essentials, you have the choice to consume less than you produce (or produce more than you consume) and create a surplus. Get ahead in this way just once, and you can ensure you won't be distracted from good investment decisions by the need to gasp for air.

Delaying Consumption Is an Emotional Ability

In the Stanford marshmallow experiment, researchers placed a marshmallow in front of a child and offered a choice: Eat it now, or wait 15 minutes and get two marshmallows to eat. Children who waited longer for the greater reward, and thus accepted delayed gratification, had better long-term outcomes in life. They were more successful, and even took better care of their health than those children who shortchanged themselves because they couldn't wait to consume the marshmallow.

The ability to delay gratification to get more of what you want in the long term sits at the core of sound investment thinking. Investment is all about accepting less now in order to have more later. If you consistently choose the path of delayed gratification for greater long-term return, you will do very, very well.

This isn't easy. It can be truly uncomfortable, even painful, to delay gratification and invest in your future. Dieting and exercise, years of night school, attending psychotherapy, working two jobs, launching a business on a shoestring—these can be difficult short-term pains that lead to really big long-term gains.

It's natural to feel a pang of loss or deprivation when saying no to consumption, and having to wait for something we want. Tell a small child they can have that delicious candy *after* dinner, and their frustration and disappointment may bring tears. Effective investors learn just the opposite emotional reaction. They smile like a baby with a lollipop when they get to invest resources for an abundant return in the distant future, and they feel like crying when they are forced to consume resources in the present that could have been invested. I think a rich imagination, a focus on the future, and a bent toward optimism enable investors to bring the emotion of the long-term results into their present decisions.

Fundamentally, delayed gratification requires a belief in abundance, and optimism about the future. It rests on a belief that there will be enough, that there will be more, that the consumption we forgo today won't be lost to all time, and that the system works and the returns will come back to us.

Future-focused investors don't feel deprived when conserving resources to invest; they feel deprived when consumption steals from their investment resource pool. I don't go to bed at night feeling sad that I had to play for the long term instead of binging on consumption that day. I'm genuinely thrilled to get to play the game this way.

Limiting Consumption Does Not Mean Limiting Spending

Katie is a friend of mine who owns a growing business in the beauty industry. When we talked recently she was deciding whether or not to carry an entire product line from a major makeup manufacturer. She liked the quality, and her knowledge of her business provided a solid basis to believe the product would sell. If it sold well, it would produce a truly stellar return on her investment in initial inventory.

We worked through the numbers together, and there was no denying they looked good. Trouble was, the manufacturer required a big up-front purchase. The size of the check she'd have to write made her nervous. I think she was wise to consider carefully before spending such a large amount of cash.

We talked about the difference between spending that amount of money on consumption and spending that amount of money on a stellar investment opportunity like this product line. Stretching to spend a lot of money on a great investment is a good move. Stretching to spend a lot of money on a shopping spree or other consumption is a very bad move. The two are opposites. Katie saw this clearly, and she chose to spend that cash on that big investment. It still felt like a big risk, but her clarity about consumption versus investment allowed her to make an intentional choice rather than an emotional one.

I know a lot of people who grew up in families that valued frugality and taught their kids to limit spending. Many of these families were frugal and responsible consumers of their income, and not active as long-term financial investors. As a result, those children-turned-adults carry an internal compass that warns against spending a lot of money. Unfortunately, that type of internal compass tends to point to "spend less" no matter which direction its bearer is facing. A better compass points to maximum return instead.

Here's an extreme example. Imagine a farmer who limits spending on seed in order to save money. As a result he plants only half his acreage in crops. Of course he doesn't end up "saving money" at all, because he eliminates half of his farm income that year by limiting his spending. He was limiting *investment*, not consumption.

Of course no farmer in the real world would be so shortsighted. The business owner that limits spending on a needed expansion, the family that limits spending on retirement investments, and the student that limits spending on learning resources are all making a decision to limit investment. It's not as obvious as the farmer who plants half his crop, but the principle and the results are the same.

From time to time I remind the managers who run my businesses that I am eager to spend money—when it's an investment that pays a good return. Because we have limited consumption and created a cash surplus from the beginning, we don't need or want to conserve cash. We want to hunt for investments that pay a good return, then quickly and happily write checks for those investments. Expensive factory equipment that will earn back its value in two years? Yes, please—sign me up.

Investors see consumption and investment in contrasting colors. They learn to cringe when they write a big check for consumption, and rejoice when they write a big check for investment. They don't operate on a simple rule of "spend less." They stretch to spend less on *consumption*, and *more* on investment.

Be Frugal About the Right Things

By limiting your consumption and investing more, you'll be directing your resources to where they can grow. When making financial investments, watch out for investing expenses that, ironically, can consume a significant slice of your returns. Perhaps consumptive expenses seem out of place in the world of investment, but I assure you that Wall Street is not populated by charitable organizations. They earn fees and commissions in a number of ways. It's their right to do business in those ways, and it's your right to avoid nearly all of those expenses.

When you buy or sell a stock or bond through a financial broker, you'll pay a commission on each transaction. Major online brokers currently charge about $7 to $10 per trade. When investing small amounts of money—say $1,000 at a time—this amounts to about 1 percent of your investment on the buying end, and another 1 percent if you sell the investment soon after. Active traders who frequently buy and sell tend to earn about the same returns as the average investor, before commissions, and a little less after paying those commissions. You can avoid paying much commission at all if you make few transactions, and hold on to your financial investments for a long time. Whether or not that's your strategy, be aware of the commissions you're paying every time you buy or sell.

Be even more wary of paying anyone a fee to manage your investments. In the typical arrangement, the investment manager takes a fee of 1 percent of the value of the investments they are managing for you. They take this fee every year, so they make money whether you did or not. Stock markets have returned about 5 to 10 percent per year on average. If your wealth manager takes a 1-percent fee, they are taking 10 to 20 percent of your gains each year, even though you are taking 100 percent of the risk and providing 100 percent of the capital. Due to the exponential effects of compounding, this can reduce your total investment returns by one-third or more over the course of a lifetime.

Theoretically, they are making investment decisions that produce above-average returns for you, but it's mathematically impossible for them all to be above average. Very few asset managers have a genuine advantage over the rest of the market, though some are lucky for a few years. If they make investment decisions that produce below-average returns for your investments, they still take their 1-percent fee.

Also be careful about mutual fund fees. Many mutual funds do something like the investment managers we just talked about. They pay a professional manager to manage the fund, and that and other expenses typically add up to 0.5 to 1 percent of the fund's assets every year. Mutual funds provide a valuable service by allowing you to own part of a broad pool of investments, thereby increasing your diversification. However, some funds' fees are much higher than others. It pays to shop around and pay attention to fees, to minimize the costly drag on your total returns.

You can get almost exactly average returns by investing in index funds that own a little of everything. Some index funds that track the broad stock market charge fees as low as 0.1 percent. Using index finds you'll probably beat most mutual funds, and pay much lower fees.

Do limit your consumption. Don't be stingy with your investment budget. Do be stingy with your investment expenses.

Beware Sunk Costs

There's another common fallacy that sometimes comes under the heading of saving money. Though intended to avoid waste, erroneous thinking about sunk costs often leads to poor decisions.

Sunk costs are resources already spent, that you won't get back no matter which path forward you choose. Here's an example.

If you invest four years of time and $100,000 in a college degree in one career, then discover that career pays less and is less enjoyable for you than another career choice, should you switch? Should the fact that you've invested so much in that degree have any bearing on the decision?

Intuitively most of us want to say yes, because it's so disappointing to "waste" the investment of four years and $100,000 by switching careers. That $100,000 investment is a sunk cost, and economists look at it this way. If the first career will pay $200,000 less over a lifetime than the second career, then sticking with the first career will cost $200,000 more than dropping it now and switching to the second. The $100,000 expense for completed college cost isn't recovered in either scenario, so it should not influence the decision. Only the difference between the two scenarios, *going forward,* is relevant.

In one of my businesses we recently spent more than $2,000 to replace the radiator and the exhaust on a forklift. As soon as those repairs were completed, we discovered that the same forklift also needed an expensive new carburetor. The $2,000 already spent plus the cost of the carburetor replacement added up more than the forklift was worth. Did that mean we should stop spending money on repairs and buy a new forklift? No. The $2,000 was a sunk cost. Whether we completed additional repairs, or junked the forklift, we would not get the $2,000 back. If we had known about the carburetor repair *before* we repaired the radiator and the exhaust, we would have decided to junk the forklift. Once the $2,000 was spent however, it was no longer relevant to the decision.

The rational way to evaluate the carburetor decision, ignoring sunk costs, worked as shown in the table on page 68.

The $2,000 just spent on radiator and exhaust doesn't factor into those calculations, because no matter what we decided to do at that point, it was already gone and not coming back. I'm happy for any chance to spend $1,200 for a $2,500 increase in value, so we replaced the carburetor.

Item	Amount
Cost of radiator repair (sunk cost):	$2,000
Value of forklift as it is now, with a broken carburetor:	$500
Value of forklift after carburetor replacement:	$3,000
Value increase from carburetor replacement ($3,000-$500):	$2,500
Cost of carburetor replacement:	$1,200
Gain on carburetor replacement:	$1,300

Say you buy an investment for $10,000, and the value drops to $8,000. If someone offers you $9,000 for that investment, should you sell for $1,000 less than you paid? It's intuitive to resist, not wanting to take a $1,000 loss on the investment. Truth is, when the value dropped from $10,000 to $8,000, you already lost $2,000. That's a sunk cost. When someone offers to buy it for $9,000, they are offering you a chance for a $1,000 gain, and you should probably take it. Like continuing to bet on a bad poker hand because you've already bet a lot, how much you "have in it" is irrelevant.

The same logic applies to years spent at a bad job, or in a bad relationship. Additional years of misery do nothing to redeem the years of misery already incurred. Two wrongs don't make a right. Confront and make change, even when you have a lot invested in the way things are.

As relational beings, we are prone to get attached, and we are wired to resist accepting losses. Attachment to people is a healthy and essential part of being human. And still, some human relationships are worth ending.

Acting like you're married to your investments is a big mistake. You'll make better decisions when you see sunk costs for what they are, and leave them out of your investment decisions. You can't change the past. Choose the option that will produce the best result from this moment forward.

Action Points

▸ See vivid contrast between consumption that reduces resources and investment that grows resources over time.

▸ With optimistic vision and future focus, develop gut-level positive emotion about investing resources, and resistance to future-robbing consumption.

▸ Do whatever it takes to create a surplus of cash and other resources so you can stop focusing on survival and prioritize long-term returns in your decisions.

▸ Spend little when the returns will be little. Spend a lot when the returns will be a lot. Limit consumption, but *maximize* investment.

▸ Be stingy about incurring trading commissions, asset management fees, and other investing expenses that threaten to skim away a huge slice of your returns over time.

Engage Online

Download a spreadsheet and experiment with how savers outpace consumers over time at *www.aardsma.com/investingbook*.

5 >   Measure and Choose With ROI

For a few months after moving into that old Main Street building, my single employee and I spent our workdays at our folding table desks by the front door. We continued to create and sell software plugins to the user base I had stumbled upon. Sales were strong, margins were high, and overhead was low. That combination meant profits were high, too.

Though my lifestyle was below middle class, I wasn't about to consume these newfound profits. My wife and I continued to drive 10-year-old cars, and put elbow grease into projects like replacing plaster with drywall in our 100-year-old house. I was quite happy with my lifestyle and didn't feel any urge to change it. I was really happy building my business and enjoying my work. I didn't feel deprived. I did accumulate cash in savings.

This raised a question: what to do with that savings? To begin, I calculated how much we'd need to set aside each year to cover our retirement. We were in our 20s, so we didn't need to save much per year to cover our future needs. The growth we could expect in our savings over time meant the annual contribution required would be small. We put that amount (a few thousand dollars) into S&P 500 index funds in Roth IRA accounts. This left a lot of savings available to do something else with.

I didn't have any good ideas for what to invest that savings in. I knew I could put it in the general stock market and make a modest return over time. That sounded kind of boring to me, and I wanted to do more with my newfound enjoyment of building my own business. I had conviction I could make higher returns in business than in the stock market.

I wasn't rich at that time, not even close. Because I was limiting my consumption, I didn't need to be rich to have an investable surplus. I already had a "what to invest extra money in" problem.

I've never found much sympathy for this challenge from anyone, and you probably won't, either. As my resources have grown and the challenge of investing them well has also gotten bigger, the sympathy seems to get even smaller. Nonetheless, it is a very real challenge for investment-minded people to decide the best thing to do with investable resources. It's not easy to find superior investment opportunities. When you feel *this* challenge, instead of the challenge to come up with some investable resources, consider it a good sign.

Besides lacking investment ideas, I had another problem: I saw a lot of risk in the software business I had built. All of our customers were users of the same software package. We didn't produce or sell that software. We sold add-ons to it. If that software package was taken off the market, bought by a competitor, or otherwise affected by a big change, we could be out of business very quickly. The narrow niche we served made for easy entry and an obvious path to marketing. It also made our entire business vulnerable to any changes affecting that niche. I didn't like that. I am prone to excessive worry about downside scenarios. Having an employee depending on the stability of the business to pay his mortgage and feed his family added a new sense of weight to my paranoia. I wanted a backup plan, and I didn't have one.

During those months of head scratching and software selling, Phil (that first employee) and I decided to setup a recording studio. We both had gone to college for audio-visual production. He graduated, I dropped out, and we both remained interested in audio and video. We figured we'd use all that office space not occupied by our two desks for our studio.

I felt silly spending money to set up a recording studio in a town of 800 people. There would be little to no demand for recording services in our area. If that wasn't problem enough, I knew the recording studio business was facing big challenges from the decreasing cost and increasing quality of home recording. I distinctly remember telling Phil, "We'll never make any money on this recording studio." I was right about that, but it turned out to be a worthwhile project for other reasons.

I didn't see the recording studio as a solution to my need for investment opportunities. I didn't spend much money on it—certainly not the money I was looking to invest. Luckily, by exploring this hobby interest, I stumbled upon a good investment opportunity.

We wanted to ensure our studio produced recordings with quality sound. That meant we'd need to ensure the acoustics of the room were top-notch. I found acoustical engineering information online, and planned the acoustical treatments for the studio. We'd need wall panels to reduce echo, soundproof coverings for the windows, and a few other things.

A little price shopping quickly revealed that buying those treatments would cost much more than I wanted to pay. I was shocked at how expensive they were. So I decided to build my own. More online research gave me the info I needed to do that, but I found it difficult to source the materials I'd need. At that time, the only way to get those specialty acoustical materials was to find a building contractor who could special order them from the manufacturers. That's what I did. The materials came in inconveniently large bundle quantities, with expensive shipping via truck freight.

After the material arrived, I came into the office on a Saturday and built the acoustical treatments for our studio. Sawdust and fabric clippings littered the floor of our software office–turned–recording studio.

The acoustical product designs were mine, the costs were low, and I was happy with how the studio looked and sounded.

I had a lot of materials left over. I sat with my legs dangling off a big bale of rockwool batts, and admired my handiwork. It still didn't make sense to me that anything should be so hard to source. We had Google and Amazon for finding and buying things. It should be as easy as a few clicks to get those materials. I couldn't think of anything stopping me from making it that way. In the weeks that followed I started ATS Acoustics, an online store selling specialty acoustical materials with easy shipping via FedEx Ground.

I wasn't about to risk much money on an untested business idea. I used some resources I already had including the suppliers I'd found, my experience in e-commerce Website development, my experience in audio engineering, and the office space we occupied. These resources wouldn't show up on a financial statement or a loan application. I didn't have any credentials or degrees in these skills, but they were what I needed. I had enough to get started. I don't remember spending any money at the beginning except $10 to register the domain name atsacoustics.com. My leftover materials were the inventory we started with.

I was thinking about the likely returns on anything I put at risk during this untested, startup phase. The first return I wanted was a learning outcome, to find out if this business would get traction with customers. I wanted to use the smallest amount of resources that would get that done.

I was really scared. Scared that people would laugh at me if it didn't work out. Scared that I didn't have the skills or the confidence to pull this off. Scared that people wouldn't understand what made me set off in this random new direction. Scared as I was, I went forward.

Fortunately that business idea worked out well. People did buy acoustical materials from our online store, and some of them wanted to buy the finished products I'd made, as pictured on our Website. I figured we made them once, so we could make them again. I hired an additional employee to help, and there in the studio and software office, we built acoustic treatments to fill those first few orders.

The software business was called Aardsma Technology Services—ATS for short. We named the new business ATS Acoustics because we shared the same office and phone lines. When customers called we didn't know if they wanted software or acoustic panels, so we just answered the phone "ATS. How can I help you?" every time.

It was a little ridiculous really. We had to wave frantically to each other to turn off the noisy power tools when the phone was ringing with a customer on the line. Our studio was covered in sawdust and fabric clippings on a daily basis. (As expected, we weren't in demand to record any bands in there.) We used the space, people, skills, and materials we had to test the return on that business before I took much financial risk on it.

It tested well, and I turned on the spigot. Over the next several years I invested nearly all of my work time and available money into growing that business. As customers placed orders and our accounting showed monthly profits, that gave me plenty of evidence that the risk was lower and the return on investment dramatically higher than what I could get anywhere else. I wasn't about to hold back from investing in a high-return opportunity like that.

ATS Acoustics grew little by little into a substantial business. Opportunism and some luck, combined with the resources we had, led to great results. My return on investment so far on ATS Acoustics is a few hundred times greater than what I would likely have received if I had invested my time writing more software and my savings in the stock market.

At no time during any of that did I have a clear master plan. I was making decisions as I went along, with dreadfully poor ability to predict the future. Luck and happenstance played a role. At the same time, I *was* thinking about risk and return, and doing my best to make rational investment decisions with my resources.

Allocate Your Resources Based on Risk and Return

Investment is trading part of your resources for something that contributes to a future increase in your resources. Something that provides a return. Your resources are always limited. There will always be more investment opportunity than you have resources to invest. This is true of time, money, and every other resource.

Nobody has enough money to buy a big chunk of stock in every large company in the world. Nobody has enough time to study every major in college, learn every rewarding hobby, or serve every good cause. Even billionaires and people who live to be more than 100 years old run short of money and time way before they run out of opportunities to use them.

I took my young daughter to a big candy store, and gave her some money to spend on one kind of candy. This place had aisles of licorice and lollipops, chocolates and jelly beans, and much more. She walked through the store, visually scanning hundreds of choices, some mouth-watering favorites, and some she scrunched up her face at and said, "Blech." Though she was only 5 years old, she found a way to sort and prioritize all those options, and pick the one she'd enjoy most. In doing that, she said no to every other candy option, so she could spend her limited money on her top choice.

Your job as an investor is very much like this. You must sort and prioritize your investment opportunities, say no to nearly all of them, and allocate your limited resources to the very best of them. Later on, as returns come in and your resources grow, you head back to the "candy store" and repeat the process of choosing the best opportunity from what's available at that time.

Flavor and color preferences might be the qualities my daughter used to sort and prioritize all those investment options. Risk and return are the qualities you'll use to sort and prioritize your investment opportunities. You need a clear understanding of the likely return, and the risk involved, in every investment opportunity you consider. Armed with this information, you can compare one opportunity to another with relative objectivity.

The Investor's Task

Take the resources available to you

and invest them where you will get

the best return available to you.

Use ROI to Evaluate and Compare Investments

In order to compare one investment to another, you need an apples-to-apples comparison of the return from each. Return on investment (ROI) is typically stated in percent return per year, and provides that standardized comparison.

(Return per Year / Amount Invested) × 100

= Percent Return on Investment (ROI)

Many investments lend themselves to direct measurement of the return, in specific dollar amounts. For example, if you buy $10,000 of stock in Company A and receive an increase in value of $500 per year:

(500 increase in value / 10,000 invested) × 100 = 5% ROI

If you buy $10,000 of stock in Company B and receive an increase in value of $1,000 per year:

(1,000 / 10,000) × 100 = 10% ROI

Sometimes the return comes in a defined period of time that's not one year. For example, buying $10,000 of inventory that will sell in three months (0.25 years) at a $3,000 profit doesn't conveniently match an even-years time frame. We still express the ROI on that investment on a per-year basis, as an annual return. This allows straightforward comparisons between investments with different amounts of time between initial investment and the payback of returns. Everything is stated in percent return per year.

Total Return / Time in Years = Annualized Return

(Annualized Return / Amount Invested) × 100 = ROI%

Our inventory example:

$3,000 return / 0.25 years = $12,000 annualized return

($12,000 / $10,000) × 100 = 120% ROI

Some investments aren't made in dollars. They might be in time, or they might be in something hard to measure in numbers. Nonetheless the same concept of ROI applies. Estimate the value of what you are investing and the value of what you will get back over time.

Here are some examples of evaluating ROI.

Choosing a Certificate of Deposit Investment

One bank offers to pay 3% interest per year on a certificate of deposit (CD), and another bank offers to pay 4% interest per year on the same kind of certificate of deposit. Because the CDs at both banks are FDIC insured, they both involve virtually no risk of loss. It's an easy decision to allocate your money to the 4% CD rather than the 3% CD, because the 4% return is higher.

This example is easy because the ROI for each CD is guaranteed by the bank, and calculated and stated for us. In many real-life investment decisions, we must estimate returns and calculate the ROI of each option ourselves.

Deciding Which Class to Take

Resource allocation doesn't always involve money. If your community college is offering free classes on five different topics, at overlapping time slots, you might have a choice to invest your time in one of them, but not more than one. The classes don't pay a financial return, at least not directly. They provide knowledge, skills, and perhaps connections to new relationships.

To rationally decide which class to allocate your time to, you'll need to evaluate the benefits that each class will return in exchange for the time invested. If some classes require a greater time commitment than others, you'll need to evaluate benefit per hours of time invested, a non-financial form of ROI. The class with the highest benefit per hour would likely be the best investment to allocate your time to.

Benefits like skills and relationships can't be precisely quantified the way many tangible and financial benefits can. We typically can't calculate 2.75-percent improvement in relationship per hour, or 6.3 units of additional skill per class taken. Nonetheless, we can make estimates that allow us to compare non-financial returns.

Perhaps you'd look through the class outlines, and count how many job skill requirements each class would fulfill. If you estimate that an advanced class will cover eight skill requirements with 48 hours invested, and the intro class will cover just four skills, for 32 hours invested, you can make a rational decision. The return on the advanced class is one skill per 6 hours, and on the intro class is 1 skill per 8 hours invested. Even when dollars and financial securities are not involved, you can still make estimates and "do the math" to make a rational decision about what offers the best return.

Deciding Which Debt to Pay Down First

If you owe credit card debt charging 20% interest, and a home mortgage charging 4% interest, and you have $1,000 extra dollars this month, which debt should you pay extra on? Paying $1,000 extra on the credit card saves $200 interest per year. Paying $1,000 extra on the home mortgage saves $40 interest per year (probably less due to the home mortgage interest tax deduction). The return on paying down the credit card debt is greater, so that's the rational choice.

Leasing vs. Buying

A business owner of mine asked about leasing versus buying some computer servers. He expressed a desire to conserve cash and be careful not to spend too much. I agreed with his conservative instinct and suggested we analyze the lease versus buy decision based on the ROI of each option.

As I recall, the terms of the lease were three years at $260 a month to lease a server that sells new for $7,000. At the end of the three-year lease, he had the option to buy the equipment for $1,500 and keep it. The three-year lease is, in effect, a way to borrow $7,000 from the server manufacturer. Here's how we broke down the ROI.

Total lease payments (36 × $260)	$9,360
Buyout at end of lease.	$1,500
Total cost to acquire 1 server via lease ($9,360 + $1,500)	$10,860
Total cost to acquire 1 server via up-front purchase.	$7,000
Additional cost of lease vs. up-front purchase. ($10,860 – $7,000)	$3,860
Additional cost of lease per year. ($3,860 / 3 years)	$1,287
Effective "interest rate" on the $7,000 borrowed. ($1,287 / $7,000)	18%

That 18% cost means the lease would have a negative 18% ROI. That gave us the number we needed to ask the next question: Did he have access to $7,000 at a cost less than 18% per year? Could he borrow at less than 18% interest per year? Could he sell an investment that's earning less than 18% per year to buy the servers with cash? He had multiple ways to obtain the cash to buy the servers at a cost much lower than 18% per year.

Sometimes life and business present more complex scenarios that require additional logical and mathematical steps to properly evaluate the ROI. My goal here isn't to replicate what business textbooks and other resources teach. It's to emphasize that mathematical evaluation of the return on each investment opportunity enables rational decision-making.

Even if math is not your thing, don't miss the concept. Lots of investment opportunities compete for your resources. The opportunities offering the highest return, after accounting for risk, should win the competition. Rationally evaluate the ROI of each investment opportunity. Allocate your resources to the opportunities where you expect the highest return.

What's the Risk of Loss?

All investments involve risk and uncertainty, and thus the future return of any investment cannot be known for sure.

You don't know for sure what Wal-Mart's profits will be next year. You don't know for sure that degree will lead to a high-paying job, those long hours will get you the promotion, or that business you are starting will succeed.

With all investments, there's a risk you will receive less return than you are expecting. You might lose part of the amount you invested (a negative ROI), or even take a total loss.

Some investments are much riskier than others. You are much less likely to lose money investing in United States Treasury bonds than you are in an untested startup business. Rational investors accept a lower rate of return on lower-risk investments, and require a higher rate of return on higher-risk investments. For example, investors are currently willing to invest in 10-year Treasury bonds for about 2% ROI, and investors typically expect 20% ROI or more when investing in startup companies.

Risk and return are the primary qualities by which you will sort and prioritize your investment opportunities.

Factor Risk Into Expected Return

The concept of expected return allows you to compare the returns of investments with different levels of risk. Here's a way to calculate that, in a success-of-failure scenario.

(Probability of Success × Return if Success) +

(Probability of Failure × Return if Failure) = Expected Return

For example, an investment in a small pharmaceutical company with one big drug about to break (or fail) might look like this. You might expect a return of 50% if all goes well and the FDA approves the drug and a total loss on the investment if it turns out the drug is unsafe. You estimate the odds of success at 75% and the odds of failure at 25%. You can afford to lose your investment in this obviously risky company. What return can you expect from this investment, taking into account those risks?

We'll convert percentages to decimals for the math. Here it is:

(0.75 chance of success × 0.50 return if success) +

(0.25 chance of failure * –1.00 return if failure)

= 0.125 or 12.5% expected return

This math applies to a simple success-or-failure case. It's suitable for most investment decisions I come across in normal life and business. More complex math applies to situations where there are probabilities of partial success, etc. For most of us in practice, the more complex the math required to analyze the decision, the greater odds of making an irrational decision.

Many times you will need to make reasonable estimates of these risk and return values, using your best judgment of the situation. If someone could tell you the precise risk and precise return in advance, investment decisions would all be no-brainers. The in-depth knowledge to assess risk and return better than others is a big part of what makes a good investor.

Make Sure You Live to Play Another Day

If the risk is high, and the return is low, it should be a no brainer to pass on such an investment "opportunity."

Additionally, some investments are too risky to justify making, even when the expected return is high.

For example, some venture capital investments in startup businesses offer a risk/return profile something like a 10% chance of a 2,000% return, and a 90% chance of total loss (–100% return). The expected return is 110%.

(0.1 chance of success × 20 return if success) +
(0.9 chance of failure x – 1 return if failure) = 1.1
= 110% expected return

That's an excellent return, if you can tolerate the risk. I'd bet a small percentage of my assets on a single investment like that, and I do sometimes. To bet *all* my assets on a single investment like that would be foolish. Doing so would mean a 10% chance of increasing my assets by 2,000%, and a 90% chance of financial ruin.

Personally, I never want to make a bet I can't afford to lose. If an investment goes poorly, or completely bust, I always want to have ample resources left to wake up the next day and try again. Sometimes that means passing up an appealing expected return because it would require betting too large a piece of my farm, so to speak.

I've made some big bets on my own businesses, but I've never found it necessary to bet anything I couldn't afford to lose. Occasionally life does present the need to go "all in" on a business or investment in an attempt to avoid losing it. Whenever possible, I try to play my cards in a way that doesn't put me in that undesirable scenario.

All Your Resources Are in the Same Pool

In Chapter 2 we talked about maximizing returns by looking broadly at all kinds of resources we can invest, not just cash. In addition to that, we make better investment decisions when we view all our resources as one pool, rather than splitting them into separate decision compartments.

Consider this example of an investment mistake. In the morning, a fictional investor named Bob looked at his retirement account, and rationally evaluated which stock or bond to invest in. He compared half a dozen alternatives, and chose the investment with the best return. That was a stock that he estimated he could expect a 7% ROI from. He invested $10,000 in it, and took a break for lunch.

In the afternoon, Bob paid his bills. He made the minimum payment on a credit card carrying a $5,000 balance at 14% interest, and paid $1,000 extra on a credit card carrying a $5,000 balance at 20% interest.

Bob made a rational decision about which stock or bond to invest his retirement money in (the best he could find), and a rational decision about which credit card to pay down (the one charging more interest). But by treating the morning's retirement investment decision as separate from the afternoon's debt paydown decision, he failed to allocate his resources to his best available return. Assuming no withdrawal penalty or tax consequences, his best available return on the $10,000 he invested in retirement that morning was to pay off both the 20% and the 14% debt. That would save a lot more money than the 7% he'd earn from the stock investment.

When allocating your available resources, there should only be one master list of opportunities, sorted by return. Creating separate groups of opportunities and choosing within them leads to errors like Bob made.

Here's another example. Say you own two businesses, both with growth potential. You have $10,000 to invest. You determine that your first business will provide a 30% ROI on that $10,000 if you invest it there, and the second business will provide a 15% ROI. Naturally, you'd choose to invest the $10,000 in the first business. Looking at all your resources in one pool goes further than that. If there is additional opportunity to invest in the first business at 30% ROI, do you have any resources earning less than 30% that you can reallocate to the first business? If so, and the risk of loss in the first business is acceptable, it probably makes sense to make that reallocation. If circumstances permit, it might even be rational to sell the second business, and invest the proceeds in the first business.

Alternately, if the first business has all the resources it needs, do you have any resources earning less than 15% that you can reallocate to the second business? Stocks, bonds, savings accounts, or property you could sell?

It's all one pool. If necessary, reallocate your resources from lower-returning to higher-returning investment opportunities.

It doesn't make sense to pay 15% interest on a business loan while earning 3% on a CD at the bank. It doesn't make sense to pass up $30/hour overtime at work and then spend an hour mowing your own lawn to save $20 (unless you want to pay $10 for an hour of exercise and fresh air).

Sometimes there are risk differences between investment opportunities, tax consequences for moving resources from one investment to another, regulatory restrictions like early withdrawal penalties, or other barriers to reallocating assets. For these reasons, it may not be practical to move resources every time a higher return opportunity becomes available. And diversification probably means you won't put all your resources on your single highest-returning investment.

Don't break up your resources into separate compartments unless there are good reasons to do that. Evaluate your investment opportunities all across the board, and when possible, reallocate resources from low-return to high-return opportunities, even if you might normally think of those resources as belonging to two separate parts of your life. Allocate resources *between* categories, not just *within* them.

Count Taxes and Inflation When Comparing Financial Returns

Unlike many investments of time and other resources, investments involving money are usually affected by taxes and inflation. The purpose of financial investment is to grow your resources. Your resources grow by the amount that's left over *after* taxes and inflation. If you compare returns without adjusting for taxes and inflation, you might make investment mistakes.

For example, if you have a choice between purchasing an investment in your Roth IRA that yields 6%, or loaning money to your friend's business for 7% interest, you must consider the after-tax returns to make an accurate decision. Investments in a Roth IRA grow tax free, so your 6% return will still be a 6% return after taxes. Interest income on the business loan you made will likely be taxed at ordinary income tax rates, currently up to about 40%. That 40% tax would change your 7% return into a 4.2% after-tax return. All of a sudden putting the money into your Roth IRA doesn't look so bad. It's as if some of the candy in the candy store is subject to sales tax, and some isn't.

Similarly, say I want to attend a seminar for my training and development, and I have two choices, each costing $1,000. One seminar qualifies as a business expense, and one would be a personal expense. The expense for the business seminar would reduce my business income, and thus reduce my taxes. The personal seminar would cost $1,000 after tax, but the business seminar would cost me only about $600 after the $400 reduction in my income tax bill is accounted for.

The type and timing of taxes is also impactful. Currently capital gains taxes on investments aren't due until the investments are sold. If you hold them for 50 years, you can delay that tax bill for a very long time, and earn additional returns in the meantime on money that would have gone to taxes. Also, currently in the United States, higher tax rates apply to gains on investments held for less than a year than on those held for a year or more. The rules tend to change. Learn how they affect your investment decisions.

Inflation also has an effect. We tend to think of dollars as fixed value things, and that's adequate for everyday life. When investing and receiving dollars over long times spans, we need to account for the change in their value over time. As is the case with all other resources, the value of currency, including dollars, is variable. Central banks try to maintain a positive rate of inflation of about 2 percent per year, which means the value of a dollar—what you can buy with it—typically goes down about 2 percent per year.

Inflation changes the value of money over time, and that means it affects the return on investments that pay back in dollars after a period of time. Most financial investments fall into this category, and are affected by inflation.

For example, if you invest $10,000 in stocks, and 20 years later sell those stocks for $30,000, your total return before inflation was 200%. If during that time inflation averaged 2% per year, it would take about $1.50 at the end of that 20-year period to buy what $1.00 would buy at the beginning. The real return, after inflation, is 200% divided by 1.5, which equals 133%.

Inflation works against lenders and most other types of investments, but it works in favor of borrowers. When you borrow money in today's dollars, and pay it back in the future with the future's dollars, inflation means the dollars you paid back with are worth less than the dollars you borrowed. Part of the interest rate you pay when you borrow money goes to cover inflation, which is not a real cost to you, and not a real profit for the lender. The remaining interest is your true cost of borrowing. For example if you borrow money at 4% interest, and inflation is 2% per year, you true cost of borrowing is 2%, not 4%.

The combined effect of taxes and inflation determine your actual return on investment, and your actual cost of borrowing. Under current rules, home mortgage interest and interest expense within a business are typically tax deductible. If my interest rate is 4%, my marginal tax rate (including state taxes) is 50%, and inflation is 2%, my true cost

for borrowing money through my home mortgage is 0 (4% interest ×
50% tax savings = 2% minus 2% inflation = 0%). The 50% tax savings reduces my rate to 2%, and 2% inflation reduces the real rate I'm
paying to 0.

Just as inflation reduces the real cost of borrowing, it also reduces
the real return on lending. When you receive interest on a bond, or an
increase in the dollar value of a stock, your real return, the increase in
purchasing power of your resources, is *after* inflation.

Again, I won't try to replicate the in-depth study of these topics
made in textbooks and online learning resources. Just remember to
consider the effects of taxes and inflation on all your investment returns.

Action Points

▸ Evaluate and understand the ROI you can realistically
expect from every investment opportunity.

▸ Include the risk of loss in your evaluation of ROI, and
compare apples to apples based on expected return.

▸ Avoid risking more than you can afford to lose on a single
investment.

▸ Sort and prioritize your investment opportunities with the
highest expected returns at the top of the list.

▸ See all your resources as part of one large pool, and make
one large list of opportunities so you can allocate resources
across and between areas of your life and/or work.

▸ As much as is practical, allocate your resources to the
highest-ROI investments at the top of the list, and say no
to all other opportunities.

▸ Include the effects of taxes and inflation in your evaluation
of ROI.

Engage Online

Find links for further study on analyzing ROI at *www.aardsma.com/
investingbook.*

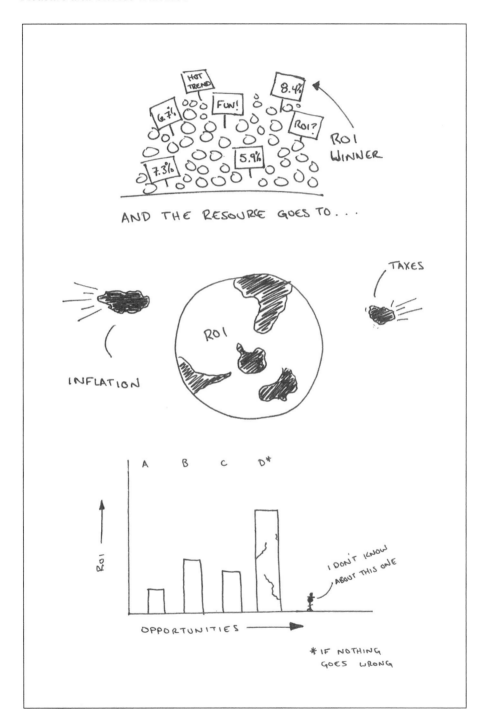

6 > Invest in Your Investment Advantages

On my first day of self-employment, when I sat down at my computer in that creepy old basement, I had some investment advantages. Though I felt foolish for starting in such a jerry-rigged fashion, and quite uncertain about the future, I had in me more advantages than I knew.

When I was 7 years old, my father brought a computer home from a university project. He showed me how to set it up and explained some things about it. Its homemade case looked like a shiny aluminum box. This was before the Internet, before Microsoft Windows, before graphical displays and color monitors. It had the aluminum box, the text-only terminal monitor, and a keyboard. I was fascinated and curious.

The only programming that computer could understand was assembly language, direct instructions given to the CPU in short abbreviations and hexadecimal codes. So I began to learn how computers worked at the lowest level. There was no manual, no help screen, and no Google. I had whatever my dad told me about it, and whatever I could figure out. I had a lot of time on my hands for figuring out. I learned how CPUs talk to RAM, how registers work, and other technical nuts and bolts. I didn't get very far, but already my advantage was growing. I was developing skill foundations that most other 7-, 8-, and 9-year-old kids didn't have. It wasn't just the computer skills. I was also learning to manage the frustration of not knowing the answer yet, to generate my own creative ideas, and to solve confusing problems without a manual or someone to lead the way.

When I was about 10 years old, my dad brought home another computer from work. This was an IBM 8086. It had a 10 MB hard drive that was about the size of a microwave, and Microsoft DOS. My dad also brought me two manuals: one for the computer, and one for Microsoft BASIC, an early computer programming language.

At the time I had one older and four younger siblings. My dear mother had her hands full and then some. My dad had a career and projects of his own. Partly by choice, partly by necessity, I was a lonely kid with a lot of time to fill. My computer gave me something challenging and intriguing to fill that time with.

Over the next eight years I spent thousands of hours learning how to write code. During that time computers became more common in homes, and improved to include color monitors and the Windows operating system. I outgrew Microsoft BASIC, and learned to code in C and C++. I didn't have much social life, or many healthy relationships, and those were not good things for me. At the same time, I was getting better and better at those computer skills. It wasn't genius that gave me that advantage, it was countless hours of practice, debugging, and repetition. I didn't know it, but I was investing all that time developing what would become one of my biggest investment advantages.

Using an advantage is the only reliable way to achieve above-average investment returns. I had some advantages, and I'm quite sure you do, too. Like me, you might not be aware of some of your advantages, or readily see how to use them to increase your returns. I want to encourage you to explore in ways that uncover and engage your advantages.

When I was 18 and finished with high school, I found a job writing software for a small business. This was another opportunity to expand my skills. It was the height of the dotcom bubble, and my small employer had big dreams of riding that wave. Like most of the dotcoms, it didn't work out. I learned some important things about realistic business models and sound management practices while watching that go painfully awry.

I used the money I saved during that year to start college at Moody Bible Institute. I planned to study radio and television broadcasting. As a new freshman in big-city Chicago, I found a lot to take in. I don't remember much from the first few weeks of college except unlimited cafeteria food, a steady stream of classes and homework, and a lot of pretty girls I didn't have the nerve to talk to.

Once I settled in a bit, I knew I'd need a job to make ends meet. One day in chapel we heard a presentation about a new software system the students would be required to use. Moody placed great value on students doing volunteer work in the community. This new Web-based system would be our way to report that we had met the requirement each week.

The system looked homegrown, so I guessed somebody around campus was developing software. I was interested. I still didn't understand the investment advantage I had developed in my thousands of solitary, nerdy hours. I just knew I needed money for school. Maybe I was also looking for something safe and familiar in the strange new world of college life.

That day, after classes, I found Moody's IT department. The corporate-looking glass doors said "INFORMATION SYSTEMS" and had a keypad for security. I had a moment of self-doubt, but it was too late to turn back. The receptionist said, "Can I help you?" and I said, "Yes, um, I'm a student here and a programmer and I'm wondering if you have any jobs for programmers." Next thing I knew I was in the VP of information systems' office. I didn't even have time to panic appropriately. He asked me what programming languages I knew. Feeling uncertain and inadequate, I defaulted to the truth: "I haven't done much, just assembler and BASIC and C and some SQL." Luckily for me, that VP was a kind man, and their entire enterprise ran on a C-based mainframe system. He offered me a job that day.

So after classes every day I went to work writing software for my college. The Internet was becoming a thing, and they wanted me to work on Web-based software that would work together with their mainframe system, what we call cloud computing now. I didn't know anything about Web-based software, so after work I walked to a bookstore in downtown Chicago and bought a book about it. Learning new programming skills from a book was a familiar and comforting path. I think I read most of that book that night in my dorm room.

My new bosses were wonderful people and healthy leaders. With their warm support I created a Web-based fundraising management system used by their nationwide network of radio stations. I learned more software skills, and more than that I learned about good business management, leadership, and what it's like to know you are believed in.

What have your life experiences taught you, that you might put to good use in your activities? We each have unique experiences that lead to unique advantages.

Following that project, I was assigned to create an enterprise-wide Web-based budget visibility system that every manager in the Moody organization would use. It was a high priority of the school's president, and got me working with people way above my pay grade. The school's top accounting people answered all my questions about the current accounting system, and accounting in general. I had a lot of questions. I gave them a real-time budget management system. They gave me an education in financial accounting, and a paycheck. We were both thrilled.

A few years later, when I sat down for my first day of creepy basement self-employment, I had no degree in computer science. I had no degree in anything. I didn't have much money, family connections, or a lot of other things. I did carry with me some important advantages. I had deep knowledge of computer programming. I was well familiar with solving problems through my own initiative and creativity. Thanks to my great bosses at Moody I had begun to understand accounting, management, leadership, and business.

My advantage of advanced computer programming skills enabled me to trade my time for money at a high hourly rate. Even better, I could use those skills plus some business insight to create products and earn much more than an hourly rate. I didn't have much of an advantage at investing in stocks, or doing physical labor, or a bunch of other things. I invested my resources where I did have an advantage: in a software-related business.

Investment Advantages Increase Your ROI

Maybe you have advantages that are similar to mine, or maybe your learning and circumstances offer a very different set of advantages. What resource or combination of resources do you possess that can increase the ROI on your investment of other resources?

Years of training as a heart surgeon allow that surgeon to earn a higher return on time spent doing heart surgery than she could earn without that training.

A complete kit of wrenches and sockets is an investment advantage that will increase the return on time spent repairing cars.

A strong network of relationships in a community of venture capital investors is a resource that allows an investor to access more and better deals and thereby receive a higher ROI from venture capital investing than he would without those relationships.

Knowledge from thousands of hours spent studying large public companies is an advantage that might allow an investor to make better stock purchasing decisions and thereby receive a higher ROI investing in those companies than he or she would without that deep knowledge.

Access to an employer-matched and tax-advantaged 401(k) retirement account is an advantage that allows many workers to earn a higher return on their retirement savings than they could without access to that 401(k) plan.

A well-developed personal ability to maintain rational judgment during times of emotional stress is an advantage that might enable superior returns from investment opportunities such as a career in leadership, emergency aid work, or financial investment during troubled economic times.

In Chapter 4 I argued that your job as an investor is to take your available resources and invest them where you will get the best return. Investing your resources where you have the greatest investment advantages will likely lead to your best returns.

The heart surgeon is not likely to get her best returns doing carpentry. The auto mechanic is not likely to get his best returns working without his tools. The salaried worker is not likely to get his or her best returns by skipping the employer-matched 401(k) contribution.

Our investment advantages and our best ROI opportunities often go hand in hand. To maximize your investment results, you must know and develop your investment advantages.

We all have advantages, and we all have resources. We aren't all investing our resources in the opportunities where we have the greatest advantage.

Competitive Advantages Enable Above-Average ROI

All investment advantages increase returns, but not all investment advantages lead to above-average returns. Competitive advantages do that. Competitive advantages are investment advantages *over other investors* in the same type of opportunity.

Learning how to do plumbing might raise a worker's hourly wage, but only doing plumbing *better than most other plumbers* will allow that worker to earn above-average returns doing plumbing.

Learning how to analyze corporate bonds might raise an investor's returns, but only analyzing corporate bonds *better than most other analysts* will allow that investor to earn above-average returns investing in bonds.

Competitive advantages make consistently above-average returns possible.

Competitive advantages are important in business and financial investment activities in free markets. With free and equal access, investors quickly jump on investments that provide above-average returns. As a result, the above-average opportunity is smoothed away by supply and demand.

For example, if a publicly traded company shows superior growth and earnings prospects, investors will immediately bid up the price of the company's stock, until the likely return on that investment is in line with the average returns from most other stocks. Information is released to all investors at the same moment, many smart people analyze it, and there's no easy way to have an advantage. Supply and demand bring returns back to the average.

The same happens in private business. If a particular town is short on donut shops, a donut-loving entrepreneur might see an advantage in starting a donut shop there. For a while, his new shop would likely experience above-average returns as the donut-deprived local population keeps the cash register ringing. Supply, demand, and free markets mean another entrepreneur is likely to hear all those cha-ching sounds and start an additional donut shop across town. This will continue, until opening a new donut shop there no longer promises above-average returns, and the advantage will be gone, not just for the last entrepreneur who opened a shop there, but for the first one, too.

If one investor has a competitive advantage over most others, he or she can receive consistently above-average returns, even in free and efficient markets. For example, if an investor does deep research to understand and correctly interpret the growth prospects of a publicly traded company before other investors catch on, that investor can get in early and earn above-average returns. This is easier said than done, because predicting the future is risky business, and there's a lot of really smart competition out there doing the same thing. Nonetheless, it is possible to generate a competitive advantage in this way.

If one donut shop has a secret family recipe for undeniably tastier donuts, they may be able to sustain more cha-ching at the cash register, despite their competitors' best efforts to lure customers away. Because competitors quickly and easily imitate most practices that result in improved business, it's not easy to sustain a competitive advantage. Keeping a secret recipe a secret is easier said than done. When businesses do achieve and sustain competitive advantages, the returns can be lucrative. When they don't, there's no basis to expect an above-average return.

Many people participate in financial or business markets looking for superior returns, but do so without developing or applying a competitive advantage. This is a recipe for disappointment. Markets themselves don't create advantages for you over other participants in those markets. The very fact that they are free markets means you have no unmerited advantage. You gotta earn it.

Though not easy, it is absolutely possible to have an advantage in a free and efficient market. To do so, you must be willing or able to do different things than most other participants in those markets. This in turn, means you must possess combinations of resources that they don't have. These could be skills, relationships, emotional stability, patents, tools, or many other types of resources.

As investors in open markets, the burden is on us to develop advantages and bring them to the table. If we don't do that, we have no right, or reason, to expect above-average returns.

Invest Your Resources to Develop Investment Advantages

Invest resources in developing genuine advantages. This will increase the ROI you can earn on your other investments, and dramatically improve your long-term results.

Your investment advantages are likely different than mine. They may include your expertise, your personality, your relationships, and others. Maybe you are worried you don't have any significant investment advantages. Don't despair. It's possible that like me, you have more than you give yourself credit for. And most investment advantages aren't handed out at birth, leaving the unlucky out in the cold.

You may not have a lot investment advantages, but you certainly have resources that you can trade for them. You can trade your time and money to learn a skill. You can trade your time and employ your relational skills to build genuine relationships that create investment advantages for you and the other party. You can trade your money for tools. You can even trade your time, energy, and money for training and development experiences that change you, as a person, and give you new advantages as a leader, an artist, a financial investor, or a philanthropic world-changer.

Invest your existing resources to gain new resources that give you an investment advantage. Develop investment advantages, on purpose. Like a woodcutter who spends part of his time resource to sharpen his axe, these can be extremely high-ROI investments.

The next seven chapters of this book will each look at one broadly applicable investment advantage that you can develop and use.

Watch Out for Advantage Illusions

Ironically, what comes to mind most readily when we think of investing—stocks, bonds, commodities, and other things traded on financial markets—are some of the hardest investments to have an advantage in. As a passive investor who buys stock in a company, but does not participate in management, set company strategy, or otherwise personally get involved, most of your personal resources are excluded from providing any benefit. For example, a trustworthy and kind person surely has an advantage over a dishonest and abusive person in many endeavors, but they each will receive the same return on the same stock purchase.

To achieve superior returns in major financial markets, you must select better securities than most other investors, or you must choose the timing of buying and/or selling better than most other investors. Neither one is easy to do, because you must compete against a large number of very smart and well-resourced professional traders and investors. There are some ways to beat them, but it's not as easy as it may seem.

A tip about a hot stock is not an advantage. If someone had truly valuable information to tip you off with, it would probably be illegal insider trading to act on it.

News stories about what a big company is doing, public information on an industry trend, or simple facts about a complex business are not advantages. Seeing a trend everyone else sees is not an advantage. If you don't have significant information other investors don't have, or have a superior way to analyze that information, then the information you have is not an advantage in public financial markets.

It's virtually impossible to predict the short-term movements of markets. It's extremely unlikely that you can determine when is a good time to get in or get out. For most of us, looking at charts and technical market measures will not bring superior insights to those generated in milliseconds by Wall Street's computers. The investment required to generate an advantage here is far more than a weekend warrior reading financial news or studying charts. Investors who consistently outperform in public markets tend to do things like spend most of their waking hours reading company financial statements and dry annual reports. This is intense work; there's nothing easy about it.

Starting a business doing something you enjoy is not an investment advantage, but it might be a good reason to identify or develop an actual advantage in that business.

Access to the same foreclosed real estate listings as everyone else is not an advantage, but training on home-inspection techniques and personally examining the properties more thoroughly than other bidders probably would be. Generalize the concept in this example to the arenas you invest in. What can you do to develop an honest-to-goodness advantage?

It's okay to wade into an area for the purpose of learning and developing an advantage. Just do it with the smallest amount of resource investment that will accomplish your learning goals. Make your experimental investments small ones.

Most of the advantages I can think of take serious time, energy, and sometimes money to develop. In a free and competitive society, there are no easy ways to get ahead. Admitting you don't have all the advantages you wish you had can be disappointing. The good news is there are hard ways to get ahead that work very well. The sooner you focus on areas where you can develop a genuine advantage, the better.

When Low Returns Are Your Best Opportunity, Accept Low Returns

An investment advantage increases your return, and a competitive advantage can lead to above-average returns. Sometimes, you won't have a strong enough advantage to get high returns from a given resource, or even any advantage at all to apply to it.

For example, without specialized skills, most workers won't have an advantage that allows them to earn high wages for their time. In this case the investor's task is still the same: to take the available resources (in this case time) and invest them where they will get the highest available return (perhaps an entry level job).

Without extensive study and practice of financial investment (maybe even with such study) most of us won't have an advantage that allows us to earn above-average returns on our stock and bond investments. In this case, the best investment for the available resources (money) might be a stock index fund that provides almost exactly average returns. Average returns are much better than putting that money under a mattress and making zero.

If you don't have a way to get more than the going rate for your rental property, rent it for the going rate. Earn that return while you work on generating an advantage you can apply to your rental house, or sell that house and move those resources to an investment where you do have an advantage.

Low returns still compound to a great deal over time. Don't refuse to make base hits because you only want home runs. Make a sober assessment of your investment advantages, and put your available resources on your best available opportunities. At the same time, build your future by investing in developing skills, experience, connections, personal character, reputation, and other investment advantages.

Action Points

▸ Take a broad inventory of all your resources and look for ways to combine them to create investment advantages.

▸ Seek opportunities to invest your resources where you can apply your advantages and receive your best available returns as a result.

▸ Look for advantages in private opportunities with personal involvement as an alternative to passive investments through major financial markets, where advantages are limited and competition is fierce.

▸ Rely only on advantages that are based on your willingness or ability to do things most competing investors can't or won't.

▸ When the best return you can get from a resource is a low or average return, accept that return and invest it, rather than earning zero.

▸ Invest resources in developing investment advantages that will increase your future returns.

Engage Online

Browse and contribute to a big list of investment advantage ideas, take a thought quiz on discovering your investing advantages, and share your thoughts at *www.aardsma.com/investingbook.*

7 > Build Yourself and Your Network

As my businesses grew, cracks started showing up in me.

I sat on the curb outside my business, watching the ambulance pull away. My heart was still beating fast. We had to call 911 to deal with a medical and/or psychological emergency in an employee whose life and health were in chaos. It wasn't caused by work, but it sure affected work. That was way more drama than I wanted for one day, or any day. I felt so stupid. That employee was the worst hire I'd ever made, and I knew it. Why didn't I listen to my own better judgment in the interview process? By making bad hires like that I hurt my businesses financially, and I added stress all around me.

On another day I walked back to my office feeling rattled and defeated. I'd gone into the factory to ask a severely underperforming worker to focus on work and pick up the pace. I brought up the issue timidly, and when he seemed to be getting angry I just walked away. I'd planned to be clear and say, "I need you to meet these performance standards in order to continue to have at job our company." Instead I avoided the confrontation that needed to happen. By failing to confront unacceptable performance, I cost my businesses money every day. Why didn't I stick to my guns?

On many days, after everyone else had gone home for the day, I'd sit in my office staring at the charts showing upward trends in sales, employee count, product offerings, and profits. Instead of simple satisfaction and gratitude, I felt anxiety that somehow this whole enterprise was going to come crashing down. I didn't feel qualified. My anxiety hurt my quality of life, and because of it, I didn't take the risks that would have maximized the growth of my businesses. Why didn't I have the confidence to take on my competitors, win, and feel good about it?

There's one answer to all these questions: My character as a person had cracks and gaps. I hadn't developed the core abilities I needed, as a person, to make the decisions and take the actions that would improve my quality of life and my investment returns. I was smart enough, and strategic enough, but my personal, emotional, relational development was a problem.

At the same time, I had another problem: I didn't have relationships with mentors and peers to reach out to when my own resources and my own character were not enough. I hadn't developed connections to a network of personal and professional supports. I was far too isolated to be healthy and live up to my potential. The solitary computer programmer didn't have what it took to be an effective CEO. I was in trouble.

These cracks and gaps in me, and my lack of relational network, were disadvantages that hurt my investment returns.

One Saturday I started reading a book about healthy, connected relationships. The book included stories from a personal development event for business leaders. I was intrigued, and I Googled the event to see if it still existed. It did, and there was one coming up in two weeks on the other side of the country. I went.

I'd never been to anything like this. I'd never even traveled by airline before. At the week-long event I learned about character, emotional intelligence, leadership, and personal growth. We interacted in small groups all week long. We learned about how we came across to the rest of our group, and how we could grow. This week cracked the door open to a whole world of growth and development I'd never known before.

I became a voracious consumer of growth resources. Once a month I flew from Illinois to California for the Leadership Coaching Program. I found a great psychotherapist and went consistently. I hired business coaches and talked to them weekly. I learned about myself, and better ways of leading. Over years, my isolation began to diminish, and the cracks and gaps in my character began to fill in. As a result, my businesses reached new levels of growth and profitability.

The growth of my businesses would have been stunted if I hadn't worked on myself. The dysfunctions of the leader become the dysfunctions of the organization. I was the bottleneck, and when I grew, the businesses grew. I spent a lot of money and a lot of time on my growth, and I made that money back 100 times over in increased business results.

I invested in myself, and built into me the character to face the demands of the roles I was filling. In addition to improving my quality of life and the quality of my relationships, I grew into a person and a leader that made me one of my own greatest investment advantages. I am still investing heavily in my own growth because I love to grow, and the ROI is off the charts.

Your Character as a Person Affects Everything Else

As an investor your job is to decide how resources will be used. Your health and maturity as a person affect every decision you make. Rational judgment during emotional stress, discernment of integrity and motives in others, perseverance during difficulty, the ability to form trusting relationships, and many more abilities flow from personal character. These personal abilities underlie successful investing.

It's not enough to be smart and strategic. No matter how much you know, a person (you) still has to do it. A person has to maintain judgment and resist clicking the "sell" button when markets are shaken. A person has to manage fear and show up at the firing meeting with a difficult employee who needs to go. A person has to manage envy and wait patiently while others overindulge in debt-fueled consumption. A person has to establish connections and build trust with key business partners. Smart people who know better still make a lot of bad investment decisions.

Your personal character, what you are capable of as a person, is a central resource, and a potentially powerful advantage. It's easy to access the same financial news articles as everyone else. It's not easy to react in mature and balanced ways to emotionally provocative economic events. It's easy to contact sources to raise capital for your business. It's not easy to build a trusted, credible connection that wins the deal. When your development as a person enables you to do difficult things others can't or won't, you have an advantage that's hard to imitate.

You can be your own biggest advantage.

Invest in Yourself, on Purpose

Significant personal growth doesn't happen automatically through the routine of daily life and work. Even dramatic life events don't usually change a person's core character. It takes an intentional, active practice of investing in yourself to raise your personal capabilities to new levels.

As an adult, you are responsible for arranging for your own growth and development. You must be the CEO of your own growth. Nobody is else going to take that role in your life, nor should they.

Personal growth happens through relationships. Intentionally pursue relationships with people who are for you, personally and professionally, who take a no-judgment approach, and who tell you the truth without sugar-coating. The best relationships for your growth and development are no-shame, no–B.S. zones.

It usually takes money for therapy sessions, seminar registrations, plane tickets, coaching fees, and similar resources to engage in the personal growth process. It certainly will take a big investment of your time. Growing yourself might be the highest-ROI investment you can make.

Take Initiative to Engage in Growth

A life coach isn't going to knock on your door and invite you to start working with her to take your career up a notch. The organizers of a workshop focused on just the skills you need probably don't know you're the perfect attendee to market to. Good mentors are typically busy, successful, and in demand. They probably won't come looking for you.

When we are very young, we have a right to expect our caregivers to take initiative to ensure we get the growth and development experiences we need. By the time we reach adulthood, that right has fully expired. Healthy development requires us to transition to taking that initiative on our own behalf. Some of us struggle to make this transition, and can let time go by waiting for opportunities and growth resources to come to us. We all need to get out of our passivity, and get active as lifelong leaders of our own growth and development.

Here are some practical ways to do this that have been fruitful for me.

▸ Reach out to people you admire. Make contact with authors, business leaders, or trailblazers in your areas of interest. Ask for time with people who embody personal and professional characteristics you aspire to. These may be prominent figures, or relatively unnoticed individuals behind the scenes. It takes courage to take the initiative and ask for a connection. In my experience, successful and admirable people are almost always motivated to pay it forward and build into others who are earlier on the path. Many people "above my pay grade" have generously shared of themselves with me. Be brave and make the ask. Sometimes this will involve you paying for a coaching or consulting relationship. I've found this works well and is worth it.

▸ Read. You can learn a great deal from the stories and insights others share in books and articles. Learn about the experiences of others doing what you want to do, or struggling with what holds you back. This is not a substitute for relational growth experiences, but it is a valuable complement.

▶ Engage with groups of peers. Most industries and interests have affinity groups or cohorts of various kinds that you can join. Support groups exist in most cities focused on addictions, emotional struggles, or difficult life events. Take the initiative to find and explore the resources that fit your need. Evaluate the quality and suitability of those resources for you. "Together" is a powerful force. Get around people who value growth, and your growth will benefit.

▶ Look for conferences, workshops, and similar events that are relevant to your growth goals. Travel a long distance if you need to. Take the initiative and make the investment. In addition to valuable content, attending events also provides opportunity for new relational connections, and focuses your time and attention on the forward motion you want.

▶ Invest in a few best-friend relationships. Everyone needs an A-team of two to five close friends. If you have some acquaintances that you see potential for a deeper relationship with, take the initiative to invite them to coffee more often. Courageously lead the conversation to what's really important in your life, which probably means risky and vulnerable topics. Most people need this just as much as you do, and will respond positively even though they might not take the initiative. Over months and years of consistent investment, those relationships can grow to provide remarkable mutual benefit.

▶ Hire a professional. Professional life coaches, business coaches, psychotherapists, personal trainers, and other helpers are accessible even when your network of connections is small. Professional helpers can devote time more consistently to working on your goals than most friends can. And professionals may have greater experience and insight to share than your peers do.

Evaluate and Develop These Personal Abilities

As you engage in growth resources, build your awareness of specific personal abilities you want to develop. These abilities are highly relevant to your investing success, and group into a few broad categories. Take a look at yourself in these descriptions. Look for relevant resources and ask for specific help with these from your growth-promoting relationships.

The Ability to Connect

The need for human connection is wired deep into us. When we connect well, we earn the trust of others and learn whom we can trust. Connection requires attuning to emotion in yourself and others, and responding with empathy. Connection depends on relating vulnerably to others, and responding gently to their vulnerability.

I've known many smart, strategic, and driven leaders who benefitted when they improved their ability to connect. They bravely practiced the art of speaking from the heart, not just the head, and speaking vulnerably about their own weakness and failure. They learned to attune and respond to the emotional content, not just the practical content in what others were saying. They learned to connect with and express their own emotion. Their effectiveness and their quality of life improved.

The ability to connect has a direct bearing on your investment returns. A healthy ability to connect helps to build teams, evaluate partnerships, make sales, and resolve conflict. Any activity that involves interacting with people benefits from this ability.

Connection is essential for another reason. It's how you get what you need. Connection gives you what you need to recover from loss, take on scary challenges, and keep your perspectives realistic and grounded. Your brain comes alive in the context of social connection.

Your resilience, courage, creativity, and energy all improve when you are well connected.

These skills are learned and practiced in relationships, whether one-on-one or in group settings. Spend time in honest relationships with people are who better at this than you are, and you will absorb their skills.

The Ability to Confront

Connection brings us closer to others. Confrontation gives us the ability to be different from them at the same time. It's based on a strong definition of oneself. Confronting is at the core of enforcing standards, saying no to a sales pitch, making an unpopular leadership decision, or holding an opinion that's contrary to the majority view. Business itself, engaging in a competition for a market, is an act of confrontation.

We all probably know people who are remarkably clear and defined. They say yes without resentment, and say no clearly and respectfully when they want to. People like that enjoy more peaceful and aligned life experiences, and people around them benefit from their clarity and strength.

Without this ability you'll be taken advantage of and overpowered by people around you. Most of us are naturally conflict-avoidant, and thus our lives and work can benefit a great deal by strengthening our ability to confront. Grow in this area to be clear about what you want, and say no to what is unacceptable or simply not your best choice.

Your healthiest and most growth-promoting relationships will support your freedom, your strength, and your clear "no." Spend time in those relationships to strengthen this ability. Push outside your comfort zone to practice it. Your investment returns will benefit when you have a strong ability to confront.

The Ability to Accept Bad Things

This is the ability to respond honestly and realistically when faced with negative realities in ourselves, other people, and circumstances around us.

None of us likes it when bad things happen. An investment loss, a personal failure, a disappointing performance by a team member, or simple bad luck can all bring out an ineffective response in us. We might deny that it's bad, see it as turned all bad, rationalize that it's not our fault, blame and criticize, or insist on perfection.

Maturity in this ability means embracing the truth when things go badly, no matter how uncomfortable or disappointing it may be. Without this ability we hang on to losing investments too long, fail to adjust what's not working, or give up on one imperfect person or investment after another in search of a new "ideal."

Life is a mixed bag, and mature adults accept that and function effectively within that reality. This is something you can work on in your personal growth contexts, if you need to.

Investing in relationships, in financial markets, in business, or in any other area requires taking the good with the bad. Investors who do that well generate superior returns, financially, in relationships, and in all endeavors.

The Ability to Be in Authority and Under Authority

Human development involves changing from a child, to an adolescent, to an adult. Children know they aren't equals with other adults, and default to a lesser position. Adolescents often push against authority, testing the limits. Adults have the flexibility to take on roles in which they cooperate with authority, and roles in which they are the authority. This ability also relates to the development of specific expertise, and finding one's purpose and calling.

Investors who take a child position might lack confidence in their own views, be susceptible to manipulation by others, or shrink back from competitive situations.

Investors who take an adolescent position might have insufficient regard for rules and regulations, or take too much risk in the face on reasonable warnings.

Adults don't automatically submit just because someone wants them to, and they don't automatically rebel just because someone is in charge. Instead of a default reaction, adults make values-based decisions about the most appropriate and effective response in any given situation. They can say, "I'll follow your lead on this" when that's appropriate, and they can say, "I'll take the lead on this" in situations that call for it.

Investors need the ability to cooperate with authority, and exercise their own personal authority, to maximize their success.

The Ability to Create Endings and Let Go

Sometimes it's time for a good thing to end to make way for something better. As humans we are wired to hold on to things, to preserve attachments, and to avoid losses. This tendency is useful in many arenas, but it's too simplistic to guide wise investment decisions.

If you can't end your attachment to an investment, a business, an employee, a relationship, or a good-but-not-best activity, you'll get stuck.

Sometimes big losses early in life, or highly impactful losses at any stage of life amplify our natural tendency to hold on to things. Sometimes we view the world as a place of shortage and scarcity, and we try to hold on to everything out of fear there won't be enough to go around. Working with your growth resources to heal and gain confidence will increase your ability to let go of things and make space for new and better things.

Healthy people and effective investors know how to say hello *and* goodbye.

The Ability to Stand up to Dangerous People

Some people are wise, are responsible, and listen openly to feedback. Some people only learn the hard way. Other people are malicious and willing to intentionally hurt others for their own gain. You need the personal character abilities to respond effectively, and differently, to each of these.

If you naively assume everyone is wise and responsible, you'll scratch your head wondering why repeating yourself didn't get the message across. Some people aren't malicious, but they are irresponsible, and they need consequences, not more words.

When you encounter a truly malicious person, you must see them for what they are, or you'll leave yourself open to serious harm. When someone intends to hurt you on purpose, bring out the cavalry (law enforcement, the court system, whatever it takes) to protect yourself from them.

My mentor Dr. John Townsend and his partner Dr. Henry Cloud have written many books about personal character qualities, and how they impact personal life and professional performance. I recommend them for further reading.

I've found executive coaches and similar mentoring relationships to be invaluable in the development of my own leadership and personal character. I still have them. I also work with entrepreneurs and other leaders as a business coach. Much of that work focuses, directly or indirectly, on the development of personal character in these and other areas.

A Trusted Network Is a Precious Resource

Earlier this year I received a phone call from a business owner interesting in selling his company to me. Though I'd never met him, the first thing he said was, "The president of my bank told me I could trust you." I was struck in that moment by the immense value of a network of trusting relationships. I got access to a deal I never would have known about otherwise, and I had an advantage before we even started talking.

Your relational network connects you to resources that can support your weak points, help solve problems, or assemble a team to tackle a project that's bigger than one person. Your relational network can provide encouragement, a foot in the door with a supplier or partner, or the support of an influential person in government or your industry. And the benefits are mutual. Networking relationships are two-way streets with no losers.

At the other extreme is isolation. Isolation is deadly. In isolation we are limited to our own resources, and we begin to lose perspective on reality around us. A lone ranger approach is a recipe for disaster.

A valuable relational network is not just a bunch of people who know each other. At its best, it's a bunch of people who *trust* each other. Trust is the core of intimate relationships. It's the lifeblood of teams performing toward a common goal. It's the heart of making a sale. It opens the door to opportunities of all kinds. Without trust, everything in business and in relationships grinds to a halt.

When I visit the drive-through at McDonald's, I hand the cashier my money at the first window, then drive forward and pick up my meal at the second window. If we didn't trust each other, I might demand to see the food before I hand them the money. They could demand the reverse, and a silly standoff would occur. Even something as simple as that drive-through transaction only works because of trust.

Your reputation is the sum of the trust people all across your network place in you. A "brand" is another name for the reputation of a business. A trusted reputation is a tremendous asset in all kinds of investment activities. It's *the* advantage for many prominent figures in business, investing, public speaking, and many other ventures.

Invest in Your Relationships on Purpose

Like other resources, a valuable and trusting relational network is something you can build. Networks like that are built through engagement and trustworthy behavior.

Engagement is making the choice to reach out, to say hello, to start conversations with people not knowing how they will respond. It's genuine interest in others, without a specific agenda. It's choosing connection over isolation, one interaction at a time.

Trust isn't sustained through presenting the right image, or crafting the right message. Trust is earned from a track record over time. Trust comes from consistent behavior.

We trust people who listen to us, tell us the truth, and do what they say they will do. We trust people who look out for our best interest even when they have the upper hand. We trust people who admit when they are wrong and do what they can to make it right.

Earn deep and broad trust by consistently doing those things. Like financial savings, trust is built a little at a time over a long time, and it can be blown quickly through bad decisions. Live in a way that makes you widely known as a deeply trustworthy person, and the network you build will be a remarkable and mutually beneficial advantage.

Action Points

- Connect the dots between your personal character and the results you get investing your time and money.

- Invest time and money in resources and experiences to grow yourself and make your personal character abilities a powerful investment advantage.

- Choose engagement over withdrawal and connection over isolation to expand your network and tap into resources much bigger than your own.

- Consistently behave in trustworthy ways to strengthen your relationships and earn the big advantage of a widely trusted reputation.

Engage Online

See a list of reader-contributed ideas for investing in your own growth, and add to it at *www.aardsma.com/investingbook*.

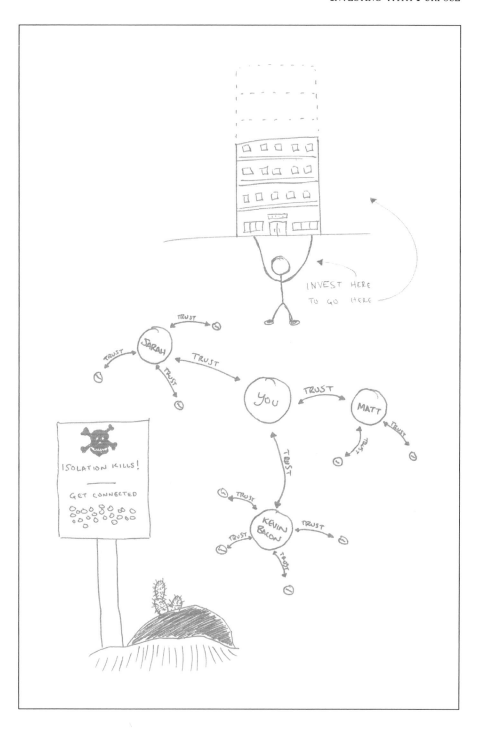

8 > Manage the Emotions That Trip Investors

My friend Gerry was having a nightmare year. After long-term success as a high-level technical salesperson, he lost his job due to changes in the market. After decades of working hard together to build a marriage and raise children, his wife told him she was leaving. His world was turned upside down. He was feeling heartbreaking pain and intense stress.

At the same time, he had a lot of decisions to make. Ready or not, he had to decide how to manage current finances, reconstruct a career, care for his children, and navigate the legal issues of a messy divorce. These were critical time-and-money investment decisions that would alter the course of his life and his children's lives, for better or for worse. The pressure was enormous.

How could he keep the grief, fear, anger, and pressure of that time from overriding his better judgment and pushing him to poor decisions with lasting consequences? It seemed almost too much to ask.

Prior to that time, Gerry had invested thousands of hours in personal-growth contexts, some as a recipient, and some as a leader. His emotional life and his relational networks were healthy. He needed every bit of that to respond to this crisis.

At the beginning, he paused. He didn't rush out and look for a new job. He didn't rush to do anything. He took a few weeks to breathe and digest what was happening first.

He paid attention to his emotion, something he is especially good at. When we talked, he would simply acknowledge all the powerful emotions he was feeling, without filtering. I know he had many similar conversations with other friends and supportive people, in which he had the same kind of unfiltered conversations. He didn't even attempt to downplay what he was feeling and the impact on him. He embraced it, and the pain that came with doing that.

Because his powerful emotions were acknowledged by him and heard by safe people, they didn't overwhelm him, at least not consistently. This allowed him to engage his rational, strategic brain in problem-solving and decision-making. With his whole brain engaged, he had the mental resources to evaluate and respond, instead of simply react.

In his decisions, he stuck to the wise life principles he had learned and taught, including principles from his strong faith. He'll be honest that he had lapses, and he didn't do everything "right." When I look back, I think he made remarkably healthy and wise decisions through that time. At the time of this writing, he's employed in a good job in his specialty, he's engaged in both the joys and the hard parts of his life, and his kids are doing very well.

Primitive Emotions Are Powerful Forces

Your brain has primitive parts and rational parts. Both influence your decision-making. As an investor your job is to *decide* how resources are used. Anything that influences your decision-making can be trouble, or it can be an advantage.

The primitive parts of our brains drive powerful emotional reactions that get our attention, give us energy, alter our body chemistry, distort our judgment, and more. Cold calculating machines, of course, don't work that way. As humans we can calculate and perform logic, but we are not calculators or computers. Emotions are part of our decision-making environment. We must respond effectively to our emotions to maximize our ability to make sound investment decisions.

Emotional reactions are rapid and compelling. They are ideal for things like urging us to jump out of the way of an oncoming train. Reacting naturally to that emotion could save your life. Reacting naturally to emotion in investment decision-making could cost you a great deal.

I'm convinced that we are much less rationally driven than we'd like to believe. The primitive parts of our brain often take the driver's seat, and our rational brains come up with reasons to justify riding along with what those primitive emotions want. It happens so quickly and so often that we aren't even aware of it most of the time.

Emotions Spread Through the Flock

When I was growing up, my parents kept chickens for fresh eggs. During the night we'd shut them in their coop, but during the day they'd roam the property.

One day I perched in one of the large trees on our property and looked down on the multi-colored flock of chickens. Brush and branches loosely covered the ground below. The chickens wandered through, picking at the ground for insects. From time to time, one of the chickens would scurry forward and flap a wing, startling another nearby chicken. In a chain reaction the whole flock would take off running, clucking, and flapping in the direction the first one had moved.

From my viewpoint, I could see there was no actual threat for them to run from, just a false alarm. From their view, all they had were signals from others in the flock that might indicate danger in the brush. They didn't stop to evaluate; they ran first, and looked around second—not a bad strategy for a group of defenseless birds on a prairie frequented by foxes and other predators. Chickens who stop to make a rational evaluation before running from a predator wouldn't fare well. Of course, they weren't on the prairie, and there were no predators in my back-yard, but they stuck with the instinctual strategy that had kept their ancestors in the gene pool.

Sometimes we act the same way. We are highly social beings. We constantly monitor the other people in the "flock" of human society for cues about our environment and ourselves. Our instincts tell us to read the flock, be scared of what scares them, and rush to snap up our share of what they are eating. Sometimes, like the chickens in my backyard, we act out of instinct in situations in which that instinct does not apply.

Fear spreads through the human flock when financial markets falter. Investors copy each other in selling the investments they are afraid of, without stopping to look around and evaluate the threat. The mood swings the other way when the flock appears to be snapping up a hot investment. Enthusiasm spreads and, like those chickens, a bunch of investors set off in the same direction, clucking smart-sounding explanations for their crowd-following behavior.

Investing is not a split-second game of life-and-death on the prairie. There's time to stop and evaluate what the crowd is doing, before deciding what you will do with your resources. We all have the herd instinct, but effective investors are aware of the emotions they catch from herd contagion, and they respond to them in ways that protect their ability to make rational and principled decisions.

Respond Effectively to Your Emotions

Effective investors are better than most at keeping their primitive brains and their rational brains online and talking to each other. They learn to be aware of what their emotions are signaling, and at the same time they stay connected to objective reality. They know how to respond to their emotions in healthy ways. They process their emotions, do the math, and evaluate the logic to check and balance how they feel. In a variety of emotional environments, they still base their decisions on their long-term intentions. Sound decision-making in the presence of emotional pressures is a major advantage in all kinds of investment activity.

When strong emotions arise, in you or in the flock, follow these steps to preserve your ability to make sound decisions.

1. Pause. Don't do anything in a knee-jerk reaction.

2. Notice and acknowledge your emotion. You can't respond effectively to emotion you ignore or deny. The emotion is real. Pay attention to it.

3. Process your emotion with someone safe. Talk about what it feels like and what you are afraid of. You can do this alone, but doing this interactively with a sane and supportive human being is much better. Give your emotion a chance to be heard and shared. That will lighten your load, get your whole brain back online, and help you regain perspective.

4. Analyze objective information. The primitive parts of our brains don't have time to process detailed information, so they ignore it. Invite your rational brain back to the party and take a look at the available information about what's really happening. Analyze and do the math, like we did in Chapter 5. $2 + 2 = 4$ during both panic and elation.

5. Stick to the rules. Times of high emotion are exactly the wrong times to jettison the rulebook. "This time it's different" is rarely true. Use time-tested principles to make your decisions during good times and bad, whether the course of action they require is comfortable or not. Base your decisions on the future you intend, the values you hold, and principles that have stood the test of time.

These steps are effective in all kinds of circumstances presenting a wide range of emotions. Here's a deeper look at a few of the big ones—emotions that cause trouble when they affect our investment decisions.

Fear of Loss

We get spooked. When something we need is threatened, we can lose perspective, and lose our nerve.

The fear might hit when a relationship you hold dear seems to be turning cold. It might hit when your employer is considering layoffs. Fear of loss would surely arise when a business you've built is showing signs it's time to shut it down and say goodbye to good years and good people. A drop in the price of a stock you bought a lot of last week could activate your fear of loss, even when the fundamental reason you bought it hasn't changed.

Fear of loss has a remarkable ability to vaporize our confidence and rationality, prompting us to retreat to a position that feels safer.

Ironically, retreat often makes a scary situation worse. Going into a fight, flight, or freeze response doesn't help any of the above situations. Sometimes scary situations are unique opportunities for bold moves, against-the-grain decisions, and taking risk to earn superior returns— not what fear feels like doing at all. Fear is a poor compass for decision-making. It often points away from our best path to the returns we want.

Sometimes fear of loss hits when things *are* going well. As a child, I remember climbing all the way up a tall tree before looking down. All of a sudden the ground looked awfully far away, and the sure-footed confidence I felt while climbing turned to shaky feet feeling for the branches on my way down. Even when we find success, we can fear how far we might fall.

Sometimes fear of loss hits us collectively. It spreads like a nervous rustling through the flock during times of economic recession, health epidemic, or political instability. The same thing often happens when financial markets drop. Sometimes we get afraid just because other people are afraid, and our anxiety can be amplified watching reporters talk in urgent tones about the latest dramatic developments.

On the whole, fear of loss is a useful instinct. It tells us to value and protect the good things we have. It drives us to stay close to our most important relationships, and protect the resources we need to survive. Due to our brain's obsession with survival, our fear instincts can be a bit overactive. To make matters worse, the primitive parts of our brains are particularly poor at distinguishing actual survival threats (the oncoming train) from negative possibilities that aren't life-threatening (public embarrassment, or a drop in market prices).

In times of fear, we are also prone to catastrophize. This is when we imagine extreme outcomes from something going wrong. It sounds something like "My boss looks unhappy. I wonder if I'm going to get fired. I won't be able to make rent. I'll be homeless in months, then I'll die alone." Or perhaps "The stock market dropped a lot this week. I wonder if the economy is tanking. I should get out of the markets while I can, before the dollar collapses and we repeat the great depression." Silly as it sounds out loud and in the daylight, we all do it. Our brains take a problem and in a split second run all the way ahead to the part where we die penniless and alone. Such moments are not the best times to decide whether or not to hit the sell button on your investments.

This tendency to catastrophize also serves a useful purpose: It gives us energy and urgency to address problems before it's too late. The young child who wanders from his mother quickly catastrophizes ("I've lost her forever!") and in distress let's out a loud wail. This serves to alert his mother while she's still within earshot, and the survival priority is once again well served.

Five hundred feet from the oncoming train is not a good time to start analyzing a time, speed, and distance equation. Sometimes the rational brain needs to step aside and let a reflex reaction address an imminent emergency.

Trouble is, our primitive brains are prone to see imminent emergencies where there aren't any. Very few investment decisions are oncoming trains requiring split-second reactions to ensure the best outcome.

If the time it takes to analyze the situation doesn't represent a life-threatening delay, you are probably best served to refrain from making decisions or changes when a sense of panic is rising in you.

As investors with decision-making responsibility, we can make expensive mistakes in a state of fear. In that state, rational judgment shuts down. We default to avoiding risk, preserving status quo, and expecting the worst. Our survival-obsessed brains don't like to take chances, even chances that are likely to lead to good results.

Reacting to a market downturn like it's doomsday is probably not in an investor's best interest. Times of widespread fear present opportunities for superior returns to courageous investors who have an emotional advantage. Good investors have a mature ability to feel fear without being overwhelmed by it. They feel the fear and retain perspective on reality, at the same time.

In January 2009, overall U.S. stocks were on sale for approximately half of what they sold for 18 months earlier. Was it rational to believe the value of U.S. companies had been slashed in half by the drop in the housing market and the recession that followed? History says no. Fear, not realistic calculations, was at work. Early 2009 turned out to be a great time to buy stocks, just as many investors were selling. As of this writing, the value of U.S. stocks has nearly tripled in the six years since then. When you read this, fear may be back in control, or enthusiasm may be winning the day. I can't predict the moods of the investing public, but I can predict they'll continue to be moody.

Fear of loss strikes us in all kinds of situations, not just when public markets get spooked. Fear of losing a relationship drives us to play it safe and avoid the tough conversations that would make that relationship better. Fear of losing a steady paycheck drives us to procrastinate on the business startup that would take our game to the next level. Fear of loss is in all of us. Sometimes fear pushes us to a wise, protective decision. Sometimes it pushes us to absolute foolishness. Fear can't tell the difference, but, using our whole brains and all of our resources, we can.

Fear of Being Left Out

We envy. We see other people who appear to be laughing all the way to the bank, and something churns in us. Their career, their results, their relationships seem better than ours, and we feel like we are being left out. Worse than that, we start to feeling like *something is wrong with us*. Deep down we fear they don't just *have* better than we have—maybe they *are* better than we are. An anxious urgency drives us to jettison what we have and go for what they have.

Danger! Investment decisions made in this emotional state can be disastrous.

At the core of envy is the belief that what we have and what we are aren't good. We fall into believing the good stuff is elsewhere out there. This implicit devaluation of our own resources is contrary to everything that makes a good investor.

When we look across town at the big new houses some of our neighbors are moving into, we might look back at our own house and see it now stripped of its "goodness" in our eyes. This is envy. An envy-driven decision to sell the house, purchase bigger, and move would likely be a very expensive act of consumption. Such a move might be contrary to the intentional future we want. Gripped by envy, we might drop intentionality and act to try to get rid of that awful left-out feeling.

When investors looked at rocketing tech stocks in the dotcom bubble of 1999, they may have felt their old-fashioned industrial stocks weren't good anymore. Those plain old stocks sure weren't keeping up with the dotcoms. Gripped by envy, an investor could easily have sold his or her holdings of solid old-fashioned companies, and bought tech stocks at the top of the bubble, the very worst time to buy them. As we all know, the prices of tech stocks crashed soon after—and still have not fully recovered, 15 years later! Those old-fashioned industrial stocks, on the other hand, have outgrown their 1999 prices by 33 percent. With hindsight and the bigger picture in view, nobody feels inclined to envy investors in tech stocks in 1999 anymore.

If an investor in 1999 had responded effectively to the fear of being left out, he or she could have gone through sound and rational analysis of the value of those tech stocks. Cisco Systems, for example, was one of the most prominent tech stocks at the time. Cisco made the routers that ran corporate networks and the Internet. The Internet was growing rapidly, and many people expected Cisco to grow right along with it.

Most stocks tend to be priced at 10 to 20 times the annual per-share earnings of the company. Near its peak, Cisco stock traded for 130 times estimated annual earnings. For that price to make sense, Cisco would have had to become 10 times as profitable almost overnight. There was no rational basis to believe that would happen. Investors weren't being rational. They were swept along with an enthusiastic crowd they didn't want to be left out of.

The crash that followed reminds us that sometimes being left out is a good thing. Sticking to sound investment principles, and doing the analysis regardless of emotional state, can remind us what we want to be left out of *before* we make the investment.

Fear of Failure

We fear being wrong, or falling short of a goal we set. We fear the embarrassment and the frustration of failure. This fear is deeply rooted in the human need to see ourselves as competent.

When we get into a new business, and it falls flat, our sense of competence is shaken. When we believe an investment is a great opportunity, and subsequently lose our shirt, we feel stupid. When we announce to our friends we are starting something new, and it fails, we feel embarrassed.

If we react to our fear of failure, we might hurt our investment returns by avoiding risk and procrastinating. Our fear of failure gives us poor guidance about risky opportunities, because it can't tell the difference between embarrassment, the cost of failure, and the cost of a missed opportunity.

Consider a new business opportunity—let's make it a taco truck—that will cost $10,000 to start up and try. If it fails, you'll sell the truck and lose $10,000. If it succeeds, you'll add a few more trucks and make $100,000 a year for at least 10 years, or as long as the taco-selling holds. You figure your business has a 20% chance of success. This is a made-up scenario, but it's not an unrealistic one in my experience.

Analyzing the ROI on that scenario, you have an 80% chance of losing $10,000 (–$8,000 expected return from the failure scenario) and a 20% chance of making $1,000,000 ($200,000 expected return from the success scenario). Overall expected return on that new business is therefore $192,000. (To keep this example simple I'm ignoring discounts for the present value of future cash flows.)

Fear of failure doesn't look at it like that. Fear of failure sees an 80% chance of falling flat and says "no thanks." That's an 80% chance of feeling like an idiot when my friends drive by my customer-forsaken taco truck. Most of us would walk away from an 80% chance of feeling that way. The likely cost of avoiding that feeling of failure is $192,000 in this scenario.

Many times, the cost of failure is much smaller than the reward for success. When we look at the odds of embarrassment instead of the expected ROI, we may pay a huge price for our embarrassment-free experience. What price are you willing to pay to avoid uncomfortable feelings?

There's another danger in fear of failure. When fear of failure strikes *after* we've made a decision or committed to an investment, we attempt to "avoid" failure by denying it as long as possible.

Jim Paul was a successful commodities trader at the Chicago Mercantile Exchange. He got attached to a big trade that eventually lost $1.6 million dollars, and cost him his job. In his book, *What I Learned Losing a Million Dollars,* he talks about the emotional factors that led to those bad decisions. One of them was the psychological resistance we all have to admitting when we are wrong. By denying his mistake as long as he could, he made the mistake much more expensive.

We all make similar errors. We hang on to an investment, a relationship, an employee, a project, because ending it will mean admitting we were wrong to get into it and we failed to make it work.

The resolution to fear of failure is not to try harder to avoid mistakes, it's to embrace the flawed reality of being human, and to integrate awareness of your flaws with awareness of your strengths. When you do that, awareness of a flaw isn't destabilizing. It's not even surprising. It's simply an acceptable part of who you are.

It's hard to take investment risks when failure isn't emotionally acceptable to you. And it's hard to take action to correct a problem when you are busy convincing yourself it doesn't exist. To make sound investment decisions you need a clear view of the good, the bad, and the ugly in your investments, in people around you, and especially in yourself.

Fear of Personal Rejection

We want to be liked. We long to be authentically transparent, and receive a response of acceptance from people around us. This fear is rooted in our deep human need for intimacy. We are wired to connect, and rejection hurts.

I was due for a radio interview in a few minutes, but I was still sitting in my car in the station parking lot. I was the day's guest on a business talk show, scheduled to talk about my new venture as a business coach. I'd marketed my companies' products for years, leading to millions in sales. That time I was there at the radio station to market myself, and it felt different. I knew I was way more afraid of this interview than I needed to be.

I wasn't feeling fear of failure. This wasn't about being wrong about going into coaching, or not generating the revenue I expected. This was about whether or not people would respond to me as a person. I was asking people to pay money just to talk to me about their leadership and their businesses. If I got no takers, or worse, someone responded with "Who do you think you are, anyway?" I'd feel personally rejected.

I pulled out my cell phone and dialed a good friend. "I've got this interview in a few minutes and I'm freaking out here." He gave me the support I needed, and I did my interview. The fearful part of me was quite surprised when I got all the business coaching clients I wanted within just a few months.

You can sit behind your computer screen buying stocks and bonds, but your best investment opportunities likely involve you, face-to-face with potential partners, customers, suppliers, or clients. Many activities involve personal selling in one form or another. Investments in relationships, learning new skills from a teacher, or seeking to do good for others' benefit—all involve risk of personal rejection. If you cross everything prone to rejection off your list, you severely limit your opportunities.

Long-term strengthening of your courage to risk rejection comes through the vulnerable and authentic sharing of yourself with people who stay safe and present even when they see your dark side. Instead of putting your best foot forward with everyone, you need some people who see the worst of you, and still accept and admire you. It's a risk to be that vulnerable, and not something to do with untested strangers. Cultivate safe and close relationships in which you can be yourself, good, bad, and ugly. That gives you the internal reserves you need to sustain an occasional disappointing or hurtful response.

The ability to go forward while feeling fear of personal rejection is a big advantage.

Fear of Boredom

We are driven toward excitement, challenge, activity, and reward. These fires burn intensely in ambitious people who read (or write!)

books like this one. Patiently taking no action for a long time can be deeply uncomfortable, and it's often the best investment decision.

Successful tree farmers understand this well. They don't grow a tree by digging it up every day to check the roots, or try planting it in a new location. They set up the growth process, and they give it time. They prune and fertilize from time to time, but most days they don't change anything; they just let the tree keep growing. Slowly and steadily, a sapling becomes a tall tree.

Good investing, in stocks, bonds, and a lot of real-life things, works the same way. If you've arranged things well, the best investment decision most days is to let everything keep growing right where it is. This isn't easy to do when you're chomping at the bit for some excitement.

CEOs are notorious for doing mergers and acquisitions driven by the thrill of the deal, not by a sound business case. Such deals tend to increase adrenaline and decrease profits.

Active traders in financial markets enjoy the daily thrill of the roller coaster. Watching real-time charts, betting this way, then that, makes it interesting. Patient, long-term investors miss the thrill ride and enjoy higher returns, on average.

Rational investing involves evaluating a range of opportunities, saying no to most of them, and allocating your limited resources to the few opportunities from which you will receive the best return. This process requires patience, inherently.

A few days before writing this section I finished evaluating an interesting investment opportunity in a unique air taxi service. After some initial checking, I signed a confidentiality agreement to obtain many pages of information. I had multiple conversations with the CEO and investment bankers on the deal. I read through obscure FAA regulations pertaining to the airline's non-traditional operating model. I imagined feeling pretty cool stepping onto flights as part-owner of the airline. I created spreadsheets to analyze the likely return on investment. And I walked away, because the numbers didn't add up.

I didn't feel a thrill when I said no to that deal and went back to the drawing board to look for another opportunity. My response was a sigh of resigning myself to more research and more analysis before I'd get to do anything exciting.

Successful investing requires patience. For some, actively meeting new people might be more fun than turning acquaintances into close friends, but investing in relationships requires a patient commitment. Moving retirement savings from one investment to another feels more active, but patience results in higher returns. Diving into a series of new learning topics might be more exciting, but completing one learning curve might offer greater returns.

If you are someone who enjoys fast-paced activity, and needs stimulating challenges, go for it. At the same time, make sure you are aware that this drives you. Incorporate those elements into your life. Fast-paced hobbies might be much less expensive than fast-paced investment activity. When you are making a new investment or changing an existing one, ask yourself if you are doing this because you need something to do, or because you have a realistic basis to expect superior returns.

Effective investors have the emotional flexibility to move decisively when moving makes sense, and to sit patiently when it doesn't.

Engage Your Whole Brain

As we've seen, the investor who can't engage his rational brain because emotions are taking over has a disadvantage. The reverse is also true: The investor who can't engage his emotional brain because rationality is taking over has a disadvantage, too.

Paintbrushes aren't good at measuring, and tape measures aren't good at spreading paint. Like an investor using emotion to make decisions, the carpenter who uses a paintbrush to measure 2x4s will have poor results. The solution is not to discard the paintbrush, of course; it's to use the right tools for the right tasks.

The emotionally powerful parts of your brain aren't good at analysis, long-term intentionality, or data-driven decision-making. They are good at some other things that make you better off with them than without them.

Emotions provide a quick signal about what's happening. Like a blinking dashboard light, they are helpful in drawing your attention to a danger, an opportunity, or a need for action. Like the "check engine" light in your car, emotions aren't good at telling you specifically what's wrong, let alone how to fix it. When the "check engine" light comes on, you need to connect the diagnostic computer to see what's wrong, and have an experienced mechanic apply expertise to recommend a course of action. But without that blinking dashboard light, you wouldn't know you have a problem until expensive engine damage has already occurred.

When an emotion sends a quick signal that something needs your attention, don't ignore it. That's like covering the "check engine" light with duct tape so it will stop bothering you. At the same time, don't react with an action before you've analyzed the situation. That's like pulling your car into the shop and telling the receptionist, "My 'check engine' light is on. Let's change the head gasket."

Engage your whole brain. Always pay attention to the signals from your emotions, *and* let the emotion prompt you to connect your diagnostic rational brain to the situation. Use that to understand specifically what's going on, and decide on a course of action. Emotions provide the signal. Analysis and expertise determine how to respond.

Emotions are useful signals, and they have another essential role that rationality simply can't fill.

My daughters like to weave bracelets and other artistic creations from small colored rubber bands. One of my daughters spent hours one afternoon sorting small rubber bands into an organizer, one color in each square chamber. After she finished, she and I both watched in slow-motion horror as her little brother toddled over, raised the organizer above his head, and shook it. A multicolored rainbow of rubber bands showered all around him. My daughter's afternoon of hard work was lost, with no way to get it back. She burst into a flood of tears.

In that moment, rationality was not the tool to reach for. My daughter needed my emotion to connect with hers and help her process this unfair and disappointing loss. My emotional empathy gave her what she needed to do that. After a few emotion-focused minutes we moved on to engage our executive brain functions in seeking a solution to the problem. That emotional connection had to happen first.

Situations like this don't just happen in living rooms, they happen in customer service call centers, college classrooms, corporate boardrooms, and investment offices too.

When the executive team is scared about a downsizing, and the CEO comes into the boardroom full of rationality, strategy, and smart ideas, the team's collective heart sinks. The CEO just doesn't seem to get what's at stake for them, emotionally. As the strategy discussion continues, their contributions are muted and their brainpower is distracted. In that moment it was not rationality—it was emotion the team needed in order to rise to the occasion and give their best to winning in a tough business competition. The lack of emotional ability in that CEO, not the lack of rational ability, was a disadvantage that would decrease that company's return on investment.

I saw another leader speaking to a group recently. He stopped right in the middle of explaining a difficult reality and said, "I feel like the room just got heavy. What are you guys feeling right now?" A few people in the room shared their sense of sadness at the unhappy ending they were facing. That leader got it. He responded with empathy, and the meeting went forward with everyone fully engaged.

Those rational parts of our brains that help so much with decision-making are useless in relational moments like these. We can't connect, relate, or lead effectively without emotion. Emotion connects you to the people you need, and the people you lead.

Don't try to apply paint with a tape measure. Don't try to measure 2×4s with a paintbrush. And don't throw either one out of your tool kit because it's bad at the other functions.

Develop and engage your whole brain. You'll relate better, you'll make better decisions, and you'll maximize your investment advantage.

Action Points

▸ Recognize when fear of loss, fear of missing out, fear of failure, fear of rejection, and fear of boredom are active in you.

▸ When emotions rise, make effective decisions by pausing, acknowledging emotion, processing emotion, analyzing information, and sticking to the rules.

▸ Use your emotion for what it's good at: signaling what needs attention, and connecting you to the people you need and the people you lead.

▸ Engage your whole brain—emotional and rational—to respond effectively to what each moment requires, and maximize your investment advantage.

Engage Online

Take a quiz on your most natural responses to these emotions at *www.aardsma.com/investbook*.

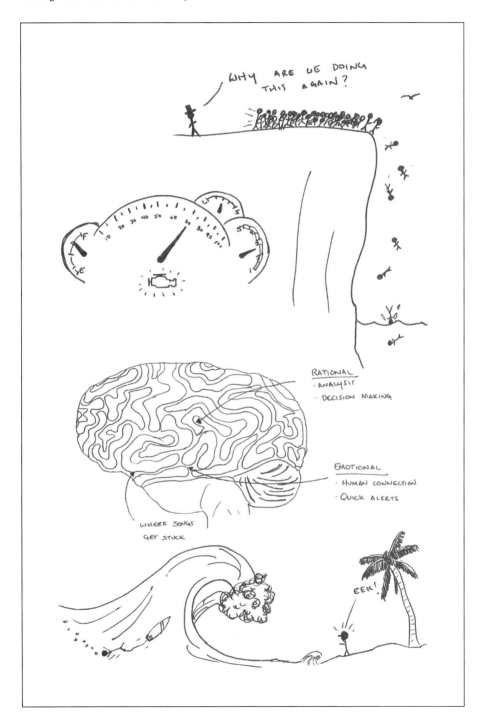

9 >   Lean Into the Difficult Work

It was a cold day in November, and it was raining. I was on the steep roof of my 104-year-old house, crouching on black tarpaper with a nail gun in hand. I was off from work to finish the roofing job before winter. I didn't have a good job or much money at the time, but I knew how to do roofing. I was saving several thousand dollars by installing the new roof myself. I was beginning to think I had taken on too much. I wasn't sure I had it in me to get it done before cold weather hit. That day I dug deep and found the energy to attack that roof. I turned on a beast mode I didn't know I had. I was hurrying, and I took some safety risks I probably shouldn't have. It was a hard day. It was snowing when I put the last few shingles on the ridgeline.

My wife worked hard on that house, too. She knocked out plaster and removed lath. She restored the century-old woodwork throughout the house one piece at a time. It was a huge, messy job: applying stripper chemicals and sanding every nook and cranny of ornate woodwork. She persisted in that long task, and the results were beautiful.

><

I knew I was about to get screamed at. The guy I had fired the day before was making a beeline for my office door, and he didn't look happy, at all.

In the seconds it took him to reach my door, I replayed the last few months of his employment. He was a good performer in sales, and gradually his drinking problem had come to my attention. When it became clear his drinking was affecting work, I sat down with him for a heart-to-heart talk. He assured me he knew he had a problem, and he wanted to get help. I encouraged him to take this seriously and consider going into treatment. The next day he asked for six weeks off to go to rehab. Feeling good about how I'd helped him to make the right choice, I gave him the time off.

When he returned, things seemed okay for a while, until one day he was caught drinking alcohol at work. I fired him. I no longer felt good about "helping" him. I'd been taken for a ride by a dishonest addict, and I knew it. And that brings us to the moment he stormed angrily into my office.

In a state of intoxication he let me have it about how I'd never believed in him, never gave him a chance, and treated him unfairly. I made it clear I needed him to leave the premises or I'd have the police remove him. He left. It was a hard day. That night I thought about becoming callous, going strictly business, no more Mr. Nice Guy. With a sigh I had to admit that I would never fit a callous way of living and leading. It just wasn't me. I'd be less naïve about addiction, but I'd continue to care and give people the benefit of the doubt. As we started the process to hire his replacement, I knew it wouldn't be the last difficult termination I'd be a part of.

><

A few months into the acoustics business, I realized we had an obstacle to overcome. Large commercial customers like schools and hospitals needed fire-resistant acoustical products to meet building codes. I hadn't designed our products with that in mind. We couldn't sell to those customers unless we altered our product designs and obtained appropriate fire rating test results.

I wasn't about to give up on selling to them, and I didn't want to go back to the drawing board with my product designs. I researched the flammability requirements and what it would take to meet them. For three months I worked nonstop on this challenge. I tested non-toxic fire-retardant chemicals and application processes. I lit test products on fire in the alley behind our building (which attracted the attention of the local fire chief). I bought a welder and learned how to use it. I sketched and built from steel, motors, and other fun stuff a computer-controlled manufacturing machine to ensure consistent quality in our fire-rated products.

During that time I could be found in the factory long after everyone else had gone home for the day. I was cutting, welding, wiring, and bolting into the night. I didn't feel bad about it. It was interesting work. I was creating an invention and I couldn't wait to see it run. As I pieced it together at what seemed like a snail's pace, I had my eye on the prize. Run it did, and after some more back-alley fire testing, we sent samples off to an expensive lab for the real tests. I waited nervously for the results, wondering if those three months of long hours would pay off. Had I calculated everything correctly? Would my design work, or would the lab tests prove I really didn't know what I was doing?

My grin was a mile wide when I got the e-mail showing we'd achieved the highest category of fire rating. Yes! Fire rating was no longer an obstacle for my business, and sales grew.

Where "Easy" Comes From

My wife and I made a lot of "easy money" when we sold the house we'd re-roofed and renovated with our own hands. I made a lot of "easy money" when I grew my businesses to a size where hires and fires became a regular part of my job. And I made a lot of "easy money" when the fire-resistant product I invented gave my company a big competitive advantage. I'm being sarcastic, of course. The path to success wasn't easy. It was difficult work.

I don't intend by telling these stories to make you feel sorry for me, as if hard work was something unfortunate that happened to me. If anything, envy me for the hard work that made me and my companies better. It wasn't easy. It was good.

There's a natural sequence in life: When you do the hard things that need to be done, your future gets easier. When you take the easy road now, your future gets harder.

When you do the hard thing and limit consumption to save and invest, paying for retirement gets easy. When you take the easy road and enjoy more consumption now, paying for retirement gets hard.

When you do the hard thing and confront a problem in an important relationship, the future of that relationship gets easier. When you take the easy road and avoid talking about it, the future of that relationship gets harder.

When you do that hard thing to learn and practice a new skill, the future of your career gets easier. When you take the easy road and avoid the difficulty of training and developing yourself, the future of your career gets harder.

When you do the hard thing and create a product or service that's genuinely better than the competition, the future of your business gets easier. When you take the easy road and offer the same product at the same price as other businesses, the future of your business gets harder.

There's potential for confusion here. You might observe a well-funded retiree, a great relationship, a well-paid expert, or a booming business and think they found an easy way that you're missing. It's very likely they didn't find an easy way; they took a hard way that others weren't willing to take, and that made their future easier.

If you try to jump directly to the easy stages those people are in, it won't work. The easy picking of fruit in the orchard comes from the hard process of planting and tending to the trees over time.

It only looks easy in the long term. If what you are doing is difficult, it does not necessarily mean you have taken a wrong turn somewhere. Lean into the difficult work.

Do Difficult Work on Purpose

In a world where individual freedom and openly competitive markets are the norm, easy ways to success disappear in an instant. If you discover a brilliant idea and begin to find success with it, I assure you a host of competitors will apply considerable time and talent to competing with your success. Imitation may be the sincerest form of flattery, but it also eliminates much of the advantage for those who went first. Soon it won't be so easy anymore. And of course, discovering a brilliant idea wasn't really easy in the first place.

To win in a competition, you need an advantage. Willingness to do easy things is not an advantage. Willingness to do difficult work is.

Professional athletes often have genetic advantages like size or speed, but I don't think you'll find any successful athlete who doesn't lean into the hard work. A linebacker who was given size and strength at birth will be outdone by a linebacker who was given size and strength at birth, *and* works hard in training and the weight room every day.

The same is true in business. An entrepreneur with a good idea will be beaten by an entrepreneur with a good idea *and* tireless execution on that idea. A financial investor with a sharp mind will be beaten by a financial investor with a sharp mind who reads a big stack of financial reports every day.

In everything you do, if you don't work hard at it, someone who does will beat you. Don't expect to find an advantage that doesn't take work.

If you want to win big, you need a big advantage. If you want a big advantage, you need to find some really difficult things to do. Looking for easy ways to have an investment advantage is kind of like looking for a fitness advantage at the candy store. Advantages are out there, but the easy store is the wrong place to go shopping for them.

I think some people give up on one difficult project after another, thinking that when they find the winning project, it will be easier than what they've tried so far. I think that's a misunderstanding of the path to winning. Tough going does not indicate you've set off in the wrong direction. Difficulty may mean you're doing something others will have a hard time imitating. That leads to competitive advantage. If your plan is realistic, and the return you expect is worthwhile, stick with it.

Look for difficult things that are worth doing. Advantages are found in doing things others find difficult to do.

What difficult things are you willing to do? What kinds of difficulty are tolerable to you that others may not be willing to take on?

Choose to Do Emotionally Difficult Things

Some projects worth doing require physically difficult work, or long tiring hours of mentally demanding work. I admire people who embrace those kinds of work when they're needed.

There's another kind of hard work that scares more people than those two: Emotionally difficult work stops a lot of people who are undaunted by a long day of exertion.

A songwriter putting her vulnerable heart into her music is doing emotionally difficult work. A scientist who dares to believe the ground-breaking solution can be found, doesn't know how yet, and still shows up to the lab every day, is doing emotionally difficult work. The leader who takes responsibility and personally promotes a vision for the organization is doing emotionally difficult work.

Fear is an invisible filter that screens out many smart and talented people. I imagine a bold red line painted in front of us all, stretching as far to the left and to the right as we can see. This side of the line is crowded, and it feels safer. The other side is sparsely populated. It feels conspicuous and dangerous.

When an entrepreneur moves from talking about a new business, to starting that new business, she steps over the red line. The crowd on the safe side gasps and shrinks back a little from the line, and a rumble of envious comments drifts through them. "Look what she's doing. I couldn't do that. I wonder if she'll make it, or fall flat." Sometimes there are naysayers in the crowd, too, yelling their messages across the line at the courageous few. "Are you sure you know what you're doing over there? It's dangerous, you know. What makes you think you can do what we aren't doing?"

The line has no guards, no fence, no barbed wire making it hard to cross. There's no requirement to be smarter, better looking, or wealthier in order to cross it. It's a line, not a fence. The few who cross it often reap big rewards, and see the futures they intended for their lives unfold in exciting ways. Back on the crowded side, people point, envy, analyze, even say it's unfair. But that powerless red line keeps them safely, invisibly, restrained.

The only requirement to cross the line is a willingness to be uncomfortable. There's no way to remove the fear so you can step into your bigger future feeling comfortable. The only way to get there is to do it afraid. Cross the line of fear that's between you and the work that will lead to the future you want.

People who won't cross that line screen themselves out. They exempt themselves from the opportunity to do the work that matters most. They prevent themselves from making changes that will rock the boat. They make sure they won't get the confidence boost that comes from facing their fears.

On the safe side of the line, there's actually a great deal of risk. Risk of lifelong discontentment in a mediocre job. Risk of your work slowly becoming irrelevant when you could have leapfrogged the industry and led an innovation. Risk of relationships that never reach their potential because you never got really honest with each other. Risk of wasting a world-changing idea by never acting on it, or watching someone else take that idea to the big time.

The price of choosing short-term comfort can be enormous, and the long-term results of staying on the crowded side of the line can be very uncomfortable.

The thing is, the one way to change your fear into confidence is to cross the line and live to tell about it. The other thing is, the "safe" side of the line actually isn't.

Everything Gets Difficult in the Middle

There's another kind of emotionally difficult work. Sometimes, and for some people, the starting is easy, but the finishing is hard. Starting a meaningful project or venture brings feelings of optimism and enthusiasm that wear off somewhere in the middle. Invariably, we encounter unexpected obstacles, and dependencies we didn't think of. Energy falters and doubt rises. Our commitment and our problem-solving abilities are tested.

I learned about this quality when I was an 18-year-old night supervisor at a grocery store. Our job each night was to unload a semi load of groceries, unpack each carton, and stock the shelves. Some nights the truck was full, and my team was short-handed. Faced with this challenge, I noticed my team would divide into two groups. One group was like the guy who sat down on a pallet of canned goods and said, "It's not gonna happen. We can't get this all done by morning by ourselves." On a night with a heavy workload that group would be *less* productive than on a regular night. I hated that reaction.

The other group had something in them that responded to the challenge. Their minds and hands got active looking for ways to step up and solve the problem. I loved that reaction. They were my allies on my quest to finish the truck by morning, come hell or high water.

When I hire people I look for that quality—that determined perseverance in the face of adversity. In the stories candidates tell, I listen for that kind of grit. Intelligence, technical skill, and people skills are all good things, but this is something different. It's what gets people through when the going gets tough in the middle.

Sometimes there's a fine line between a brick wall, and a surmountable difficulty in the middle of a big undertaking. There is such a thing as hitting a brick wall that you cannot push through. Sometimes trying to go forward in that direction will just waste resources. Don't beat your head against it. Dig under. Go around. Get a ladder. Go back and find a different road. Most of the time we give up too soon. Failure is rare. Usually it's not failure, it's giving up before reaching success.

It's really hard to know what to give up on, and what to persevere on. Only in hindsight can you know for sure what is impossible, and what is merely extremely difficult. Some questions to ask: Does this violate the laws of physics? Does this violate the laws of my country? Has anyone done anything comparable to this before? What, specifically, is the current obstacle, and what ways around it are possible? Can I back up, regroup, and try another path to the outcome I want?

Most of us are prone to give up too soon, not to persevere too long. Find a way forward. Try 14 different ways if you need to. Cultivate perseverance in the face of adversity. It's a kind of emotionally difficult work that can make or break your future. I've never seen an important project that didn't require it. Persevere, and give yourself an advantage.

How to Find Difficult Work to Do

Perhaps you are motivated and sincerely willing to take on difficulty in pursuit of your goals. Maybe at the same time, you aren't sure what difficult work to take on, or where the opportunities are.

If so, consider engaging in seeking solutions to one or more real-world problems. Tackle a problem that's holding you back in your work, or that affects other people like you. Face into a difficult problem in you as a person, and engage in a process of growth. Work on a problem that affects society, and that you have a realistic shot at making a difference to. Identify a problem worth solving, and you will find some difficult things to do. Explore possibilities with curiosity.

When you are engaged in exploration, you'll stumble on interesting things to do. Don't take a passive stance, waiting for a cause or an idea or a challenge to come to you. Look around, interact with people, notice what could be better in you and in your world. Don't wait to be asked. Select yourself to do something about it.

When you do this, you will feel fear. You may fear you can't make a difference, or the difficulties will be too much. You may feel you aren't qualified enough or resourceful enough, or in some other way not enough. You may worry nobody will notice what you're doing, or think it's important. We each have different fears, but we all have them. Sometimes "I can't find anything to do" is a mask to cover "I'm scared." We are all scared. Admit it, and go ahead with the difficult work.

There's no shortage of difficult work to be done. This world is long on difficult challenges and short on people courageous enough to take them on. Easy paths are hard to find, but difficult paths are all over the place. If you're engaging in exploration, and you are willing to attempt scary things, you will find some difficult and worthwhile paths.

Action Points

▸ Anticipate difficulty as a normal part of worthwhile endeavors.

▸ Abandon any search for an easy path to success, and instead look for opportunities to do difficult things.

▸ When the danger is more emotional than consequential, cross the fear line that most others won't.

▸ If the outcome you seek is achievable and worthwhile, persevere when initial enthusiasm fades and unexpected obstacles arise.

▸ Gain an advantage by engaging in these kinds of emotionally difficult work.

Engage Online

See other reader's ideas for difficult things worth doing, or contribute yours at *www.aardsma.com/investingbook*.

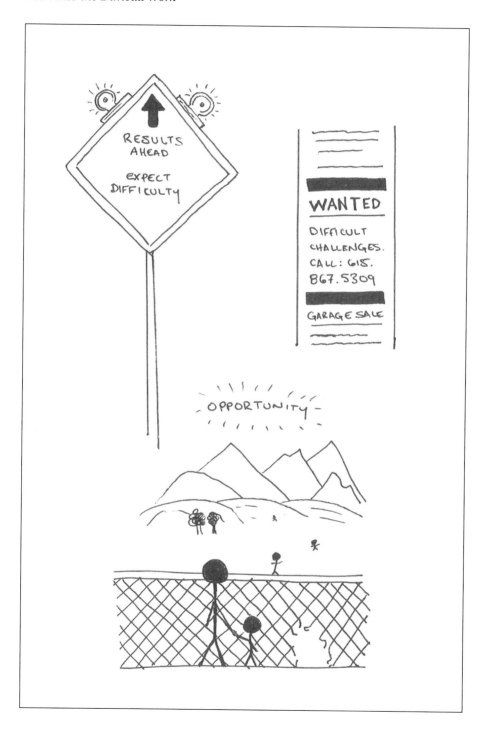

10 > Trust Homework, Not Hunches

In the second half of 2014, oil prices made a gradual and remarkable decline from about $105 a barrel to about $45 a barrel. The price of stock in Exxon Mobil, the world's largest oil company, declined steadily with the price of oil. I found it hard to resist that quality company on sale for a bargain price. I felt the price of oil had fallen too far. I admired the company as a sound business. I figured I wouldn't mind owning Exxon Mobil stock long term. I bought a bunch.

Over the next few weeks, the price of oil rose modestly, but my Exxon Mobil stock fell. That left me scratching my head. As I watched the price of oil, the price of stocks overall, and the price of Exxon Mobil stock interact, I began to understand better how multiple factors drive profits at that company. Price movements showed me that the value of Exxon Mobil didn't have a simple relationship to the price of oil. It also responded to interest rates, the value of the U.S. dollar, and especially economic expectations. I also learned more about the supply, demand, and cartel dynamics affecting the price of oil. I realized my knowledge of the oil business and the oil markets was way too shallow to make a call about oil company stock. I'd underestimated the long-term impact of factors driving oil prices down, and I'd made a mistake. I said "uncle" and sold my Exxon Mobil stock at a loss.

As investors, our job is to decide how to use our resources to produce the future results we want. My decision to allocate money to Exxon Mobile stock didn't lead to the future result I wanted. The investment was a mistake—not because I took a loss, but because I violated one of my own investment rules. I invested in something I didn't thoroughly understand.

I always think of Ed when I remember what it means to thoroughly understand something. Ed and I lived on the same dorm floor in college. He was obsessed with aviation. He approached every conversation with energy and enthusiasm, but when the subject was aviation-related, his energy went up another notch. The guy was passionate and knowledgeable.

One day my girlfriend and I took the Chicago "L" train out to O'Hare Airport, just to walk around. It was pre 9/11, when non-ticketed-passengers could still go through security. As we looked through the concourse windows, I noticed a jet with an unusual angled engine configuration. I hadn't seen that before, and I was curious about it.

A day or two later I ran into Ed in the dorm hallway, and asked him. "Hey, Ed. I saw this weird jet engine at the airport the other day. I don't know what type of plane it was, but it was angled like this. Do you know why?"

His reply blew me away. "It depends if the aircraft was made *before* or *after* May of such-and-such year." He went on to explain the history of that engine and its manufacturer, the basis for the design, which aircraft manufacturers used it during what time periods, and why. I had figured he'd know something about it, but this was over the top. I had asked him a random aviation question with no warning, and he was ready with deep and detailed knowledge about it. Something about that level of mastery thrills me, and it reminds of the difference between knowing a few facts or simple storylines and thoroughly understanding something.

The closer you are to Ed's level of understanding of what you are investing in, the better. When you thoroughly understand an industry, a company, a technology, a culture, or anything else, you have an investment advantage.

I got another reminder of this a few days before I wrote this section. I was at a social gathering with some of my wife's friends. Bill, a quiet, middle-aged man, was among the group. At one point in the conversation he told us a little about his day. Bill is an expert commercial roofing analyst. When an insurance company needs to know why a multi-million-dollar roof failed, or a building owner has a leak nobody can figure out, they call Bill. He's spent most of his life on top of buildings looking at roofs.

That day he visited a large church building with a pattern of leaks popping up in multiple places. He looked at the stains on the ceiling tiles in various rooms of the building, and then told the owner, "I'd say your roof membrane is from [manufacturer X], made between 1987 and 1991, and you had a significant hailstorm last summer." He hadn't even climbed a ladder and gone on the roof yet! His diagnosis was correct. Like the Sherlock Holmes of roofing, clues that wouldn't mean much to others were all Bill needed to solve the case.

Ed thoroughly understands how airplanes work, and Bill thoroughly understands how roofs work. When you thoroughly understand how your investments work, you have an investment advantage.

Don't Buy Simple Stories

The human brain is a meaning-making machine. We take bunches of facts and details, and condense them into concise interpretations. These stories help us simplify complex reality and give mentally manageable meaning to jumbles of information. We think and communicate with storylines.

For example, when financial markets move this way and that, we look for headlines to give meaning to the data. "Treasuries fell, the dollar fell, and stocks rose because the Federal Reserve said they might wait to raise interest rates." Ahh. It all makes sense. The perplexed feeling we had when we saw the day's price charts changes to a pleasant feeling of knowing comprehension.

The trouble is, the reality of what happened that day is much more complex. Millions of investors made buy and sell decisions for millions of individual reasons. The headline's explanation of the overall result may not even be accurate, but with the story to tame the data, we feel satisfied. Often we feel satisfied by that plausible storyline even though it completely misses the true causes of that day's price movements.

This ability to simplify observations into stories is a wonderful capability of our brains. It's necessary so we can cope with the complexity of a world filled with virtually infinite events and information. In many cases, our stories serve us well, because they are good enough models of complex reality.

We might use a simple story like "Traffic is bad so it's going to take longer to drive downtown." That's mentally manageable in a way that analyzing the number of cars on every feeder street is not. The reality of the traffic situation is massively complex. The number of people going to work today, rain or snow on each stretch of road, carpooling trends, accidents, even things like Daylight Savings Time affect the specific details of traffic on a given day. That complexity is simply too much to process, and we don't need to analyze that complexity to decide what time to leave for our theater date. We simplify, and the mental streamlining we receive in exchange for lower precision is worth it. We can round our drive time up a bit, and make the complexities irrelevant to the decision.

Other stories don't serve our decisions well. "Lawyers make a lot of money. I want to make a lot of money. I want to be a lawyer." That's a simple, mentally streamlined story, and there's truth in it. At the same time, the complexities masked by this simple story are also highly relevant to the career-choice decision. Lawyers also spend a lot of money on law school. Some lawyers discover they don't enjoy being lawyers. Some lawyers put in a lot of time as low-paid junior associates before ever making a lot of money. Current trends in the legal profession are toward excess supply, less demand, more automation, and contract outsourcing, putting downward pressure on lawyer's compensation. There's a real chance the aspiring student who sets off to make a lot of money as a lawyer, never actually will. The simple story that our meaning-making brains stamp with "makes sense" is an inadequate basis for the decision.

Lots of people recognize that a career choice is a complex, multi-factor decision, and wouldn't make such a big time investment decision based on a simple storyline. We are familiar enough with the complexities of a career choice to resist drastic oversimplification. We can protest: "But wait, it's not that simple. What about this factor?"

Perhaps we are more susceptible to trusting simple stories when it comes to financial investments in unfamiliar territory. A classic approach to picking stocks started by dividing them into industry segments, picking the strongest industry at the time, then picking the strongest company in that industry to invest in. It's a logical story that makes sense, but it didn't work. The selected companies didn't perform any better than a randomly selected stock would have. The real factors that drive company profits and stock prices are just too complex to accurately simplify into "strongest industry" and "strongest company."

"Traffic is bad" is good enough to decide what time to leave for the theater, but simple stories like "more of our electricity will come from wind and solar" aren't good enough to decide how to invest your money in energy stocks. There are many other factors that influence the future prospects of energy companies, and predicting one trend (not easy in itself) is woefully inadequate to predict investment performance.

Without in-depth knowledge to check them against, simple stories feel plausible and mentally satisfying, even when they are completely wrong. If you find yourself thinking, "I don't know a lot about this, but that explanation makes sense to me" or "This investment will do well because of one simple factor," red flag that thought. That kind of rationale is not a reliable basis for investment decisions of any kind, whether relational, financial, vocational, or otherwise.

Thorough understanding, like Ed's knowledge of aviation or Bill's knowledge of roofing, is great insurance against buying simple stories.

With that depth of understanding, it's easy to remember that reality is much more complex than a simple storyline. An expert knows what other questions need to be asked and answered to make the right decision.

Invest in Thorough Understanding

You can develop thorough understanding by investing time to research, learn, test, and practice.

Dig in to learn more. Read articles, books, executive bios, Wikipedia pages, or whatever learning material applies. You'll start to find additional simple storylines that don't agree with the first one you heard. And you'll find additional facets of the situation that are relevant.

Don't be afraid to get practice in an area you are unfamiliar with, for the purpose of learning. Just keep clear that the outcome you are looking for is learning, and the resources you are devoting are a learning cost. Get the learning for the lowest cost that will get the answers you need.

Look for ways to check the storyline in a test or experiment. There's nothing like real-world results to shatter assumptions and raise interesting new questions.

For example, if you want to learn about trading stock options, practicing by watching actual options respond to price movements is quite instructional. There's no need to wade in with real money, let alone large amounts of real money, to get that instruction. Recognize your limited experience is a disadvantage, and practice trading with a Website that offers "paper money" simulated trading. You don't need to risk real money to get the learning outcome you want.

You might learn, as I did, that options trading is harder than it looks. That lesson is less painful when your losses are in imaginary dollars instead of the real thing. If consistent results over time prove you have a real advantage, *then* risk resources in search of a financial return.

Many storylines can be illuminated through tests or experiments. If the simple story is "Consumers will love this because it has a modern design," do some test sale on eBay, or read customer reviews to see how consumers actually respond to similar products. If the story is "This company earns more during construction booms," pull some historical financial statements on that company and test your theory against the data. If the story is "This job candidate will be a great fit because his last job required the same skills," set up a working interview where you can see those skills in action.

As you dig into learning, the satisfying layers of simplicity will peel away, and confusing complexities will become apparent. "Hmm. Customers like some modern-designed products but not others." "That's strange. The company actually earned less during the last construction boom due to safety problems." "The candidate performed well on the skills, but was late for the working interview and seemed defensive about feedback." Not so simple now.

The confusion that comes from digging into new learning might be an uncomfortable feeling. We can avoid confusion by relying in ignorance on simple, sensible stories. We can also reduce confusion (to a point) by gaining deep understanding of a subject or situation. On the learning curve between ignorance and deep understanding, we have to travel through confusion. This unpleasant mental discord that comes with the learning process is a good sign. It means you are moving closer to understanding the reality of the situation, and it also serves to protect you from the overconfidence that comes from trusting a simple storyline.

You are more likely to make an investment mistake when you know a few satisfying storylines than when you are engaged in a confusing learning curve. The feeling of confusion is a valuable signal that you need to learn more before deciding. Simple stories, on the other hand, eliminate confusion without adding actual understanding, and believing them is asking for trouble.

Research and testing will dispel simple stories, and help you see the complexity you must grasp to make an informed decision. Investing the time to thoroughly understanding an opportunity will lead to an investment advantage.

Embrace Not Knowing

At one of Berkshire-Hathaway's giant shareholder meetings, I heard an audience member ask Warren Buffett and Charlie Munger what they thought about the new electronic currency BitCoin. As I recall, Munger said, "I don't have any idea about the value of a BitCoin," and Buffett said, "I don't either. Berkshire won't be investing in BitCoin, I can tell you that. We know what we don't know." Next question.

Some investments are so speculative or uncertain, deep understanding of their prospects isn't possible. Other times thorough understanding is possible, but the cost of learning about an opportunity outweighs the potential returns.

If it doesn't make sense for you to spend the time to go through the learning curve, that's okay. That probably means you shouldn't make a decision about that investment either. Effective investors frequently walk away from opportunities they don't understand.

Most investments will fall into this category for most of us. We have many opportunities to be seduced by simple storylines, and many opportunities to admit what we don't know and stay out of trouble.

As an investor, you must be able to tell the difference between the illusion of competence from shallow storylines, and a realistic basis for confidence based on deep understanding.

Learn to recognize and be honest with yourself about areas in which you don't have thorough understanding. Reject simple storylines that temptingly offer to bring meaning to that knowledge gap. Just say "I don't know." Dig deeper to learn more, or look for investment opportunities you understand better.

Understand the Lifeblood of a Business

You understand *how* a business is performing by understanding its accounting. You understand *why* it's performing that way by understanding some other things.

What's the economic engine at the core? This is where value gets created. Like the engine in a car, this is where the economic power comes from that drives everything else. In a manufacturing business it's on the assembly line, where the whole product almost magically becomes worth more than the sum of its parts. In an insurance business it might be the ability to accurately price risk, and the financial capacity to take those risks. In a brokerage business the engine at the core might be sales made through trusting relationships. Understanding the core value generator(s) is an essential part of thoroughly understanding a business.

How do people treat each other there? This is the culture of an organization. Many organizations with smart strategy underperform or fail completely because the employees, customers, or other people involved don't like how they are treated. Is it a competitive culture, a collaborative culture, or a nurturing culture? Does that culture fit the company strategy and the customers' needs?

What's the competitive advantage? Do people want what they sell? Do customers have solid reasons to choose this business over another provider? What, if anything, do they do that's hard to imitate?

All these taken together build a framework for thoroughly understanding a business. This applies to a solo business, a small family business, or a giant corporation. When you can answer these questions in an informed way, you have an advantage in making investment decisions about that business.

Understand What You Are Involved In

Our most important investments are usually more integral parts of our lives than owning stock in a large and distant corporation. With thorough understanding we'll make better decisions about closer-to-home arenas like our households, our friendships, our jobs or businesses, and our own training and development.

I review financial results from each of my companies a day or two after month end. On a daily basis I look at graphical dashboards of key performance indicators like sales, backlog, capacity utilization, and advertising response. These businesses are my most important financial investments. I keep the information to understand how they are doing close at hand.

My wife does a great job faithfully accounting for every dollar we spend from our household budget. Each New Year's day we meet to review what we spent in the past year, and decide what to budget for the year ahead. (This holiday activity may give you a glimpse into what a fun-loving person I am.) The accounting my wife does gives us the thorough understanding we need to make informed decisions about our personal consumption. Understanding via accounting enabled sound management of our household finances, which played a key role in our overall investment capability and results.

I've noticed entrepreneurship and a love for accounting sometimes don't coexist in a given individual. If you are investing in your own business, you need to understand the key accounting measures of that business. You don't need to do the accounting yourself, but you better read and understand the numbers that describe the state and performance of the business. Understanding the financial metrics of a close-to-home business is probably even more important than understanding the finances of a public company, in which more accountability and analysis are in place.

Financial investing without good financial accounting is like painting a portrait in the dark. It might keep you busy for a while, but when the lights come on, it's gonna be ugly.

It goes without saying that you need to understand the terms of a car loan, employment contract, or life insurance policy before you commit to it. Thorough understanding and wise decisions in such close-to-home financial matters often make a bigger difference than scrutinizing investments you are less personally involved in.

Understanding isn't just for financial investments. It applies to investing in relationships with people, whether friends, employees, or a future spouse. Don't rely on first impressions or simple storylines about a person's character. Seek to know people more thoroughly before you trust too much.

Understanding applies to investing in your own development, too. Seek to understand your own fears, desires, strengths, and history. Ask people around you for feedback and insight about how you behave and interact.

Take time to learn and understand beneath the surface, and you'll make better decisions.

Action Points

▸ Maintain a grounded awareness of the limits of your understanding: which investment decisions are in areas you thoroughly understand, and which investment decisions are outside of those limits.

▸ Approach decisions with extra caution in areas in which you don't have thorough understanding, but you do know enough to be dangerous.

▸ Don't be lulled into a false sense of understanding by simple, plausible storylines that mask decision-relevant complexities. Dig deeper, or admit you aren't qualified to make investment decisions in that area, and move on.

▸ Invest in attaining thorough understanding by engaging in learning. Reduce risk and increase ROI on your learning experiences by doing small-scale experiments, not big ones.

▸ Access and understand financial accounting for your household, and any businesses you invest in. Understand the economic engine at the core, the organizational culture, and the competitive advantage of those businesses too.

Engage Online

See what other readers want to do more homework on, and share your ideas at *www.aardsma.com/investingbook*.

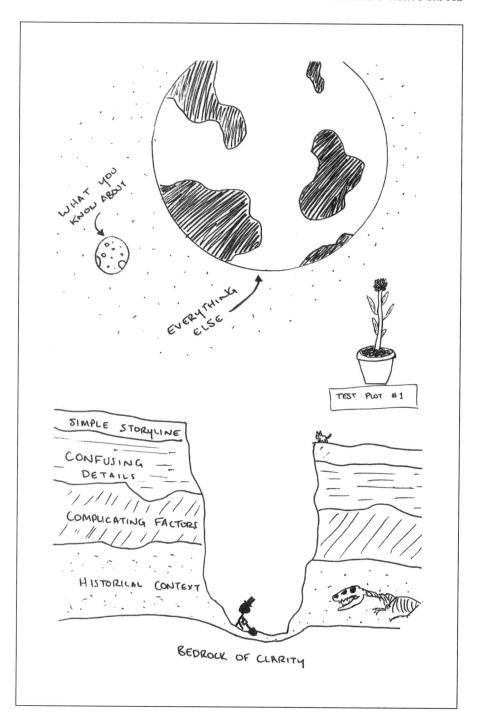

11 >   Own What You're Building

Eric spent decades honing his skills as a risk management expert. He worked for nationally recognized leaders in the field. He moved up the ladder in his career. He worked on high-profile projects. He even made career moves from one organization to another to keep advancing. Based on his expertise and experience, he currently earns a very nice salary and benefits package. He helps build the systems of the organizations he works for, and he helps protect those organizations from threats. I bet he'll always be able to find a good job until he decides to retire. He'll never lack for food on the table or a good health insurance plan. But he does not own what he's building.

Oscar also spent decades working as a risk management professional. He has certifications, experience, and connections in the same field Eric does. For years they followed similar tracks, and earned similar wages. Then Oscar made a change. He invested time and money to build a risk management system of his own. When he was ready, he took a big risk. He left his day job and started his own risk management business. He got meetings with executives at potential client businesses, and pitched his services.

Clients signed up, and Oscar installed his system at one site after another. Less than a year after going full time with his business, Oscar was earning about 10 times the money per year that Eric was. Why? It's not because Oscar is smarter, more skilled, or better trained, or has the ability to do things Eric can't. It's because Oscar chose to take the risk to own what he was building, whereas Eric continued to build systems owned by others.

Oscar added the advantage of ownership to his investment of time, and the effect on his returns was dramatic.

Owners have profound advantages.

Owners Get Paid for Taking Risk

Oscar invested time and money in his product and his business with no guarantee of success. He risked years of his life and a chunk of his financial future.

Oscar also took an emotional risk. He let responsibility for his income and his career fall onto his own shoulders. He had a wife and kids depending on him to make good. He risked failure and disappointment. He risked looking bad in front of his friends and his family.

There's yet another set of risks Oscar took. If his product malfunctions, and a client experiences losses, he could be liable. The core of his business is taking a portion of his client's risk off of them and onto his business.

A lot of the extra return he's earning now is compensation for risks Oscar took that Eric didn't.

Whether it's real estate, oil wells, farmland, stocks, creative works, or the corner grocery store, people who own those things are taking risks that wage earners aren't taking. Sometimes owners lose big time. Markets go bust. Investors can and sometimes do lose everything they invested.

As an owner, I've sometimes worked hard an entire month in a business that lost money during that month. None of my employees has ever worked for negative wages in their job.

In other months I've made more profit than any employer would pay me or my employees for a month's work. Owners take risks that employees don't, and sometimes owners get paid very well for doing that.

Some of the risks owners take are emotional, not financial. Sometimes the price of entry is emotional discomfort, not money. Because many people aren't willing to take those emotional risks, owners can earn superior returns.

The risks of ownership are often skewed strongly to the upside. Owners can decide to stop investing in what's not working, and continue investing in what is, receiving long-lasting returns on their successful investments.

Many business ventures have risk/return profiles something like the one shown in the table on page 166.

The risk profile of ownership differs greatly from the risk profile of employment. We could make a similar table comparing the risk profile of owning apartment buildings to the risk profile of renting apartments, or the risk profiling of directing a not-for-profit to the risk profile of working at one.

Many ventures with potential for huge returns start with a difficult and risky early phase in which returns are negative and the future is uncertain. The payoff for taking on that type of risk profile can be very large.

You get to make a personal choice about what risk profile you want to take on. If you look at the first few rows of the previous table, you might decide ownership is a raw deal, and employment is much safer. Many people look at real life that way, I think.

Look at the long view, not just the current year or current decade. Look at your personal characteristics and abilities. Consider taking on ownership-type risk profiles to open up big possibilities for your future.

Investment advantages come from willingness and ability to do things others find difficult. Accepting the risks of ownership is one of those things.

Event	Owner Risk/Reward	Employee Risk/Reward
Business Begins	Risks a year's wages in capital. Takes responsibility for overall business success/failure.	Risks no capital. Takes responsibility for specific job duties.
Early Operation	Loses money each month. Puts in a lot of time for an uncertain future outcome. Decides direction.	Makes money each month. Puts in scheduled time for an agreed-upon paycheck. Follows direction.
If Early Failure	Loses entire investment. Carries emotional burden of personal failure and finding a new career direction.	Loses job. Carries emotional burden of job seeking.
If Conflict Between Owner and Employee	Decides outcome. May terminate employee.	Accepts outcome. May lose job.
If Big Business Breakthrough	Receives multi-million dollar increase in net worth.	Potentially receives a modest raise of a few thousand dollars.
Sales of Successful Business	Is relieved of ownership responsibility. Receives large cash payment.	Has new bosses assigned, not chosen. May lose job.

Owners Are on the Other Side of the Labor Market

Every market has a supply side, and a demand side. Farmers grow vegetables and supply them to the produce market. Grocery stores and consumers want vegetables, thus providing the demand.

Employees supply the labor market by trading their time for money. Businesses are on the other side of the labor market; they are part of the demand for labor. Employees sell their time. Businesses buy it.

It may be to your advantage to be a buyer rather than a seller of time, for a number of reasons.

Time is your scarcest resource. Every hour you trade for money is an hour of your life you can't get back. There are ways to get a lot more money, but there are no ways to get a lot more lifetime. Employees trade away their limited time. Owners can bring in the time of many employees, building something much bigger than they could ever build alone, even in a lifetime.

Globalization is bringing billions of people into the labor market and probably allowing them to compete with you for your job, even if they live on another continent. And this additional labor is coming online at low prices. This big increase in the supply of labor benefits buyers of labor such as businesses, and hurts employees, the sellers of labor. You might gain an advantage, and do more good, by being an employer who creates a job, than an employee who uses one.

Additionally, business owners have the flexibility to hire or contract labor from any country that best meets the needs of their business. Employees don't usually have the flexibility to move to whatever country offers the best employment opportunities. Owners have an advantage in the globalizing labor market.

There's another force affecting the labor market. Not only is supply increasing, but technology is limiting the growth of demand for many kinds of routine labor. The Internet, computers, robotics, and other technology trends are increasingly automating what used to be done by employees. This creates opportunities for skilled technicians who create and maintain high-tech equipment, and removes opportunities for workers who use to do the jobs smart machines have taken over.

The business owner receives increased returns when new automated equipment welds the product together precisely and cost-effectively. Those employed as welders earn a decreased return when the automation replaces work they used to do.

There will always be job opportunities for lots of people, but already, developed countries don't have job opportunities for everyone who wants one. If you are willing to be an owner who employs others instead of seeking employment, you can participate in the other side of the labor market, and you might find a big advantage there.

Owners Participate in Markets for Goods and Services

Employees participate in the market for the type of work they do. The wage for computer technicians is determined by the supply of computer technicians and the demand for their services. A carpet installer participates in the market for carpet installation labor, and his or her wage is determined by the supply and demand for carpet installation labor.

Owners get to participate in different markets than employees do. An owner of a computer assembly company can employ those computer technicians and participate in the market for assembled computers. An owner of an apartment complex can employ that carpet installer and participate in the market for rental housing.

When I shifted from selling my time as a software developer to creating software products that I could sell unlimited digital copies of for no additional cost, I shifted from participating in the market for software development labor, to participating in the market for usable software products. The latter was much more lucrative than the former for me.

Some products and services are worth much more to the market than they cost to build. That was the case with my software products. Owners can earn that difference as a potentially large return. Employees don't usually have that kind of opportunity for outsized returns, because they are competing against many other people with the same sets of skills.

Owners get to participate in markets for goods and services that employees don't. This can be a big advantage in generating higher returns.

In addition to participating in markets for goods and services, business owners can participate in the market for businesses, by selling their business and/or buying other businesses. Significant investment returns can come through this avenue.

Active Owners Tend the Resources They've Invested

If you are a skilled and conscientious gardener with a bag of apple seeds to invest, you might earn a higher yield of apples investing those seeds in an orchard you tend than in an orchard tended by an unknown gardener of average skill and average motivation.

If you are good at business, or a certain type of business, you might earn a higher return investing your time and money in a business you tend than in a business tended by an unknown manager of average skill and average motivation.

Active ownership in your investment can take on different forms. You might be the active owner of a business, the active owner of investment real estate, or the active director of a nonprofit organization, for example.

Active owners tend to the management and growth of their own investments. Passive owners leave the tending to others. At the least, active owners pay attention to how the investment is faring and have the control to replace the manager tending to the investment, if results are unsatisfactory.

At my current level of wealth, if I buy stock in any company in the S&P 500, I won't have the clout to be an active owner of that stock. Instead I'll have a passive role. This keeps my time free, and at the same time prevents me from having any active ownership advantage. I'll get the returns of any other passive investor in that stock, but I won't have the advantages of controlling ownership, or even significant influence as a part-owner.

Active owners typically need a broader range of skillsets than employees do. The active owner of investment real estate needs skills in site selection, deal making, legal matters, hiring contractors, marketing, and managing tenants. The installer that owner employs to replace carpet in the apartments doesn't need that broad range of skills. He or she needs only to be good at one primary job skill.

If you have the desire and the ability to be an active owner, you may find a significant investment advantage in that role.

Sometimes Owners Don't Know Their Hourly Rate

When you are creating something, like a business, an invention, or a screenplay, you don't know the hourly rate you're working for. It could be negative, it could be higher than any reasonable salary. This is one of the risks owners take.

Monty Widenius didn't know the hourly rate he was working for when he started creating the computer database system MySQL in 1995. I guesstimate he spent at least 25,000 hours coding MySQL before he sold it to Sun 13 years later. That's more than 3,000 work days filled with problem-solving, fatigue, doubts, and no guarantees.

On top of that, Monty was giving MySQL away as free open-source software the whole time. He saw the long view. He wasn't playing for a paycheck at the end of the week. He lived with the risk that events out of his control might mean the long view never even came true.

In 2008 he finally knew the hourly rate: His income from the sale was roughly $25 million (source: *https://en.wikipedia.org/wiki/Michael_ Widenius*). That's about $1,000 an hour. On top of that, the software he created became a staple of the Internet software world, used by Facebook, Twitter, Google, and many more. His return went beyond dollars to worldwide recognition and impact.

If he had approached any software company in 1995 and said, "I'd like you to pay me $1,000 an hour to write database software," would any owner have agreed to that deal? No. He had to be his own owner and take a lot of risk to make that deal come true.

Business Owners Get Investment Opportunities Others Don't

Now that Oscar has his risk management business, he has exclusive access to investment opportunities within that business. When Oscar has $20,000 to invest, he can look within his business for an advertising opportunity, a new hire, or additional software development that will earn a return. It's quite likely he can find opportunities that pay 100% or more ROI. Because Oscar is the owner of his business, he doesn't have to bid or compete against anyone else for those fantastic investment opportunities. Whereas other investors would kill for a 20% ROI in public markets, Oscar can put his own capital to work at 100%+ ROI within his own business.

At various points in the growth of my acoustics business, we needed more space. To meet those needs I used some of the profits I had earned to buy existing buildings, or buy land and build a new building. I became the landlord for my own business. I got a friendly and reliable tenant (my own businesses) and the businesses got a friendly and reliable landlord (me) who put priority on whatever the businesses needed to grow and succeed.

I earned higher returns than what I could get investing in commercial real estate rented to others. My legal and marketing costs were $0, for example. And my occupancy rate has been 100% the entire time. I'm sure other real estate investors would love to rent real estate to my businesses. They don't get the opportunity. I get first dibs on investing in the real estate my businesses will occupy, because I'm the business owner. Ownership creates opportunities like that.

You don't have to be an entrepreneur or an active business manager to take advantage of the outsized returns businesses sometimes generate, but it helps. Passive shareholders in a business that has high-return internal investment opportunities also benefit in a similar way. The trouble is, you need to be an owner *before* the prospects of the business improve. The price of stock in publicly traded companies reflects investor opinions of the future prospects. Unless you have access or information that other investors don't, stock in businesses with a promising future will already be expensive. Knowing which businesses are most likely to see their prospects improve in the near future is a challenging feat.

Business owners get to invest at whatever it actually costs to build the business. Outside investors get to invest at a price that reflects the future potential of the business. A restaurateur can own a new restaurant business for the cost of kitchen equipment, inventory, etc. An outside restaurant investor will have to pay a multiple of the expected future profit to buy in. For a restaurant with great prospects, this difference could be large, giving a huge advantage to the owner/ entrepreneur.

Ownership of a successful business creates investment opportunities that sometimes return dramatically more than publicly available investments do. This may be the best financial investment advantage I know of.

Ownership Isn't Just for Profit-Making

The day I wrote this section I visited a number of related not-for-profit organizations, including Lawndale Christian Community Church

(LCCC). They are located in the North Lawndale neighborhood of Chicago. The organization's leaders have been working there for 40 years to improve a poor and difficult neighborhood.

The community of Lawndale has lacked quality housing residents can afford. Slumlords didn't share the values and priorities of the leaders at LCCC. So what did they do? They raised money, bought land, and built houses and apartments. Since then LCCC has developed more than $60 million in real estate in the Lawndale neighborhood. Some of it they rent to local residents. Some of them have sold to local homeowners. They got control over the local housing situation by becoming local housing owners. And this ownership ensures they will keep control into the future, enabling them to implement their values and priorities in the community.

The community of Lawndale had another problem: The residents wanted local access to affordable healthcare. Once again, LCCC became an owner to solve the problem in a way that fit their mission. Using donations and ultimately large federal grants, they built a medical facility that's now the size of a small hospital. LCCC owns it. They do dental, vision, prenatal care, and so forth, for affordable fees. By owning the medical facility they have a big advantage in working toward the community development future they desire.

Whether your goal is to get rich, improve the neighborhood, or save the rainforest, ownership can give you advantages that help you get there.

Own Your Work Without Owning a Business

Business ownership is a powerful path to financial investment advantage. At the same time, it's not for everyone. It requires broad skills, both technical and interpersonal. It requires a tolerance for risk and an internal drive.

If you feel business ownership is not for you, you can still benefit from owning your work. You can build and own something that's not a business, like an invention, a work of art, a book, or a physical building.

You can own productive assets like real estate or farmland without the operational complexities of running a business.

You can take ownership by forming and leading a group of people to work toward a cause, collaborate on common goals, or share industry best practices. Leaders have ownership benefits that members don't.

You can invest in developing skills that you own for the rest of your life, so you don't have to "rent" those skills by hiring others to do things for you.

You can become a freelancer, trading your time and skills for money. You'll have more flexibility, take more risk, and likely earn a much higher rate than employees earn doing the same work. I have a friend who observed at the beginning of his IT career that consultants earn far more than employees for the type of work he does, so he became an independent consultant. He's getting the benefits of ownership without running a business, at least not in the sense of managing employees and operations.

Depending on local market conditions, it may be an advantage to own your residence instead of renting it. Owning instead of long-term leasing property, like your car or tools you use, is usually an advantage. Whenever it makes sense, look for opportunities to pay one time and own a productive resource, rather than paying over and over again for the use of something long term.

If active ownership really isn't for you, you can still own small parts of businesses by buying stock in publicly traded companies. You'll have to compete against lots of other investors to buy that stock, so you probably won't get a great bargain. Still, the returns on owning and accumulating stock will eventually outpace the returns from most day jobs.

The extra risk and responsibility of owning what your building might be very well worth it.

Action Points

▸ If it fits you, consider earning higher returns than the supply and demand market for your skillset offers by investing your time and money to build and own something of long-term value.

▸ Take on the emotional and/or financial risks of ownership to open up investment opportunities that are unavailable to those who choose the safety of working under someone else's ownership umbrella.

▸ If you have the desire and the ability, access superior investment opportunities by owning your own business.

▸ Even if entrepreneurship isn't for you, look for opportunities to be an owner of your work, passive investments like stocks, and the things you use in your daily life.

Engage Online

Take a quiz on how entrepreneurship fits you and see a reader-contributed list of ideas for owning what you're building without owning your own business at *www.aardsma.com/investingbook*.

12 >   Keep Rolling the Snowball

Two years into the launch and growth of ATS Acoustics, I was getting restless. That business was past proof-of-concept, and it was generating solid profits. Its future looked bright, and I fully intended to lead it to that future if I could. At the same time my thirst for creative invention and my urge to find high-ROI investment for those profits compelled me to look for an additional business opportunity.

There were two things I knew I didn't want to do with the profits that were coming in:

1. I didn't want to consume them in an increased lifestyle. Sure, I could have sold the old minivan and bought shiny red sports cars or something. I knew that dumping those profits into my lifestyle would stop the upward momentum of my business investment. That would be like cutting down an orchard of seedling apple trees to get firewood for a fun bonfire. Decades of apple production traded in for a fun party? Never. I wanted those resources to keep growing.

2. I also didn't want to direct those resources into average-returning investments such as the overall market for stocks and bonds. That would be like planting those seedlings in a huge public orchard where competition for space is fierce, and where I couldn't apply my time and talents to creating superior growth.

If I put those resources in the public markets, they'd grow, but only slowly. I thought I could do better taking my resources and investing them where I had an advantage. I didn't need the big scale of financial markets, because my resources were still small. I needed a high ROI to keep my resources growing.

Phil, the film school graduate and original employee, still worked with me. His job had morphed from installing software modules to selling acoustic panels. (I appreciated his flexibility.) He also had a videography business on the side. One day we chatted at his desk about a large video project he was bidding on. It involved three cameras, a video switcher, and some other gear neither of us owned. He had a quote to rent that gear for 30 days. I thought the quoted price was really high.

The next morning I said, "Hey, Phil. If you get that big video job, how about I buy that gear and rent it to you for half of that quote? When you're done with it I'll either rent it to others, or sell it or something." That sounded good to him.

We both waited to see if his bid would win the job. I started to think, "What *will* I do with that gear if I buy it?" I wondered if an online rental store could work. My mind raced ahead to imagine all aspects of the business model: reservations, logistics, shipping, online marketing, and so forth. We could ship nationwide from one central warehouse, using equipment much more efficiently than local rental stores could. I started to think the business could work and I could start it using the gear I'd buy for Phil's big video project.

A few weeks later Phil found out he had lost the bid. Someone else had been awarded the big video job, and he had no need for that gear after all.

You know when you flip a coin to make a decision, and while the coin is hanging in the air, you suddenly know what you want the outcome to be? When I heard that Phil didn't get the job, it was like that for me. I was disappointed. I wanted to start that rental business. So I did.

I bought one popular, high-end video camera. I began to create the software that would handle online ordering and real-time reservations. I was engrossed in the thrilling task of taking the online rental business from dream to reality. We were still sharing the office and phone lines, so we named this one ATS, too: ATS Rentals.

Newborn ATS Rentals had an awkward problem: We only had one piece of gear in our inventory. If a potential customer came to our Website and saw our inventory of one, they'd wonder what sort of crazy startup this was and never trust us to be their rental provider. On the other hand, if I bought a full range of inventory, and the idea flopped, I'd be out serious money. I don't like to take big risks on untested ideas.

We solved the problem by listing every piece of audio and video gear Phil and I personally owned. Phil agreed if his personal gear got rented, he'd let me ship it out to the customers, and he'd get a cut of the proceeds. We then had enough categories and items on our Website to look semi-legitimate. We paid for some online search marketing and waited to see if anyone would rent anything.

Luckily the one item ATS Rentals actually owned was the first item that got rented. We got paid, and shipped it out to the customer. For a few days ATS Rentals was sold out. The camera came back. I bought another one, thus doubling our inventory. The business model worked.

Not long after that, I hired a full-time equipment buyer. Seven years later, we haven't stopped buying. ATS Rentals now owns thousands of video cameras, projectors, lenses, and other pieces of audio-visual gear. I've been able to reinvest millions of dollars of profit from ATS Acoustics into ATS Rentals at a high ROI. ATS Rentals was just the investment opportunity I needed to keep those resources growing. Thanks, Phil, for the inspiration.

Now I have a new "problem": ATS Acoustics and ATS Rentals are both much bigger businesses than they were seven years ago, and they are both generating solid profits. Because I reinvested my earlier profits, profits grew, creating even more profits that need to be reinvested.

If I succeed in the challenge to find new and bigger opportunities to reinvest all that profit, future profits will be even bigger. This is the positive spiral of compounding returns.

I intend to make investment decisions that continue that spiral until I run out of ideas, lose a bunch of money on bad decisions, or run out of lifetime. I'm hoping it's the latter, a very long time from now.

The returns I want aren't just financial. Entrepreneurship has been good to me. I want as many other people as possible to experience that rewarding thrill ride. I also want people everywhere, from the poorest on up, to value all their resources and invest them in ways that improve their lives and our world. I'm compounding my resources and investing my life for purposes like these.

Not all investment leads to compounding growth. When you assemble the right ingredients, compounding returns grow off the charts.

Allow Plenty of Time

Time is our most precious resource and an essential ingredient in the compound growth process. Start compounding as early in your life as possible. Most of the returns from compounded investing come in the last few years of the process. Start a few years earlier, and you will dramatically increase your ultimate returns.

Consider the table on page 181, showing the growth of $10,000 over time, based on 10% annual growth.

Some observations:

After 65 years of compounding, the original $10,000 has increased roughly 4,904%. That's a lot more than 10% per year times 65 years = 650%. Compound growth is exponential not linear.

It takes awhile for this process to pick up momentum. The amount earned in year 65 is about as much as the amount earned in the first 40 years combined!

Compound Growth of $10,000 at 10% Annual Rate					
Year	**Annual Increase**	**Total**	**Year**	**Annual Increase**	**Total**
0		$10,000	35	$25,548	$281,024
5	$1,464	$16,105	40	$41,145	$452,593
10	$2,358	$25,937	45	$66,264	$728,905
15	$3,797	$41,772	50	$106,719	$1,173,909
20	$6,116	$67,275	55	$171,872	$1,890,591
25	$9,850	$108,347	60	$276,801	$3,044,816
30	$15,863	$174,494	65	$445,792	$4,903,707

Assuming the investor lives until age 95 (not an unreasonable assumption in our time [*www.cdc.gov/nchs/data/hus/hus11.pdf#fig32*]) starting to compound that $10,000 at age 29 instead of age 30 will increase the total result by $445,792. If our investor starts at age 20 instead of age 30, the total result will increase by almost $8 million! Time is of the essence.

Limit Consumption and Reinvest Your Profits

Consuming $100 in year 0, instead of investing it, would reduce the overall return by year 65 by $4,904. Consumption early in the game is very, very expensive later on. Investment early in the game is very, very rewarding later on.

It's tempting to increase your consumption as your resources start to grow. Too much consumption devastates long-term results.

If our investor had decided to consume half of each year's investment returns, and invest the other half, the total after 65 years would be just $238,399 instead of $4,903,707. With the numbers in this test case (10% return over 65 years), cutting the reinvestment in half reduced the final result by more than a factor of 20.

Consumption and reinvestment are enemies of each other. Extra consumption, especially early on, will slash the final size of the snowball you're rolling.

It's almost irresistible to increase consumption as your resources increase. With my growing family and my human nature, I've only partially succeeded in my efforts to keep my consumption from growing. At the very least, ensure your annual consumption is a decreasing *percentage* of your annual income. Make sure your annual income including investment returns is growing much faster than your consumption is. This will preserve much of your compound growth potential.

It's not enough to protect your profits from increased consumption. You must also find good opportunities to reinvest those profits. This reinvestment challenge gets bigger every year. In year one our investor only needs to find an opportunity to reinvest $1,464 at 10% return. In year 65 our investor needs an opportunity to reinvest $445,792 at 10% return, a much bigger challenge.

In year one our investor could do something like upgrade to more efficient household appliances, and probably save 10% of that cost in reduced utility bills for decades to come. It's harder to find an opportunity to deploy $445,792 in household efficiency upgrades. The hunt for high-returning investments gets tougher as the quantity of resources to reinvest gets bigger.

Don't Get Trapped by Diminishing Returns

All investment activities run into limits. Every investment will reach a point at which the ROI starts to decrease as the amount of investment increases. Some investments reach that point much sooner than others.

The ROI on spending five minutes sharpening an ax before a day of woodcutting is enormous. A doubling of productivity might result. Spending an additional five minutes at the beginning of that same day (10 minutes total) sharpening that ax won't quadruple productivity. The increase in productivity might be just a few percent more. As the ax approaches the sharpest it can be, the return on extra sharpening time diminishes to zero. Ax-sharpening is a high-ROI investment with rapidly diminishing returns. It's well worth doing a little of, but it doesn't scale beyond that.

Learning a new skill is similar to ax-sharpening. Taking a class to improve your job skills might be a very high-ROI investment of time and money. Take the same class again, and your return will diminish compared to the first time. Taking a different class related to your job skills will again offer a good ROI, but take enough different classes related to your job and soon the returns will shrink again. As your skills become state of the art for your field, the return on further training diminishes to near zero. You can invest much more time in job skills than you can in ax-sharpening before you run out of worthwhile return. Skills training scales better than ax-sharpening, but it still doesn't scale from 1 to 1 million. Because you'll run out of relevant things to learn, and run out of lifetime to use your skills, a few cumulative decades of skills training is probably about all that makes sense.

Scaling a local business also runs into limitations that diminish returns. Todd's commercial lawncare business operates in a city that contains about 1,000 businesses with lawns. At the beginning, Todd only had 10 customers, and his advertising paid off really well. There were 990 potential customers out there to advertise to, and some of them wanted a new lawncare provider. As his business grew to 100 customers, then 500, his advertising became less and less effective. Half of the people who saw his ads were already doing business with him, and most of the other half were happy with their current provider. Advertising that used to generate 100% ROI now generated only 10%. Todd will receive a diminishing return on investing in growing that business in that city.

To break free of that limitation, Todd could expand to other cities, or even go nationwide. With a few million potential customers in his new nationwide market, Todd could once again earn great returns on his advertising investments. He could probably scale that business big enough to keep him busy growing for decades or perhaps even a lifetime. Eventually though, everything runs into a limit. At a few hundred thousand customers, Todd's lawncare business would once again run into steeply diminishing returns.

When you have a little to invest, small opportunities, with high ROI, that also use a lot of your investment advantages make sense. As your resources grow exponentially through compounding reinvestment, you'll need to find investments that can scale bigger without experiencing significantly diminished returns.

If employment is your path, this might mean changing jobs to invest your career time in a larger company with bigger opportunities. If you are a business owner this might mean expanding your business to other products or services. In financial investing this might mean adding investments to your portfolio that don't offer the same level of superior returns as the opportunities you found when your resources were smaller.

Your available time is a strict limit, and prevents significant compounding growth of anything that requires a lot of your time to keep generating returns. As your resources grow, it's especially important to find investment opportunities that can grow without taking up more of your time.

Investments in financial markets are the most scalable investments I can think of. These markets are so large that no individual in a lifetime could run out of opportunities to invest in them at acceptably average returns. This huge scale comes at the cost of average returns because most of us don't have advantages that enable us to earn above-average returns in large public markets.

When your resources are small, look for creative opportunities to earn higher returns than you can get in those big markets. As your resources grow, expand into opportunities that fit the scale of your resources.

Continue to Allocate Your Available Resources to Your Best ROI

The rate of return you earn each year has a dramatic effect on the overall result after an extended period of compounding. Increasing the growth rate of our investors $10,000 from 10% per year to 12% per year more than triples the total earned over a 65-year period. Earning 8% instead of 10% has a similar effect in the opposite direction, reducing the total earned by 70%.

This dramatic long-term effect is all the more reason to work diligently at allocating your available resources to your investment opportunities from which you expect to receive the highest return.

As your resources grow, your ROI on a percentage basis will almost certainly shrink. It's not that hard to invest $1,000 in something that turns it into $2,000 in a year, for 100% ROI. Pre-order something in bulk for 50% savings. Upgrade tools or equipment to increase your productivity. Advertise your freelance services. Get a skill certification that leads to a raise. Hire a personal trainer to improve your health and reduce medical costs. Hire a life coach to improve your career path and job performance. It's very difficult to invest $1 billion in something that turns it into $2 billion in a year. Search for high-ROI opportunities in the early years, before the challenge of deploying large amounts of capital sets in. Earning 20% instead of 10% in year three has the same effect on your total results as earning 20% instead of 10% in year 30, but it's a lot easier to do in year three, when the resources you need to deploy are smaller.

Compound Growth Works for Non-Financial Investments, Too

Mary was a director of a small not-for-profit dedicated to animal rescue. She worked hard to promote the organization and raise funds. She spent a lot of time meeting with potential donors and volunteers. She did a good job, but it didn't scale. She could only meet with a handful of people each day. Even if she rushed through meetings and cramped her schedule, there was no way she could double the number of people she was meeting with, let alone grow her organization to 10 or 100 times what it was.

She could break free of her time limitation and move into a compound growth scenario by reinvesting some of the donor money and volunteer hours to create a staff of PR advocates and fundraisers. If those reinvestments resulted in a net increase in resources for the organization (a positive ROI), Mary could repeat the cycle by increasing the staff further, and receiving even bigger returns.

Alternately, she could get into a compound growth cycle by creating a system in which the average supporter recruits more than one additional supporter, and those new supporters go on to do the same. That's compound growth that isn't limited by Mary's time, or Mary's network of contacts.

Any time you can use the resources you have to generate additional resources that can, in turn, be used to generate even more resources, you can get compound growth.

Don't Compound Backward

Debt has all the wonderful characteristics of a compounding investment. In most consumer debt, the growth automatically adds to the principal, making it grow even faster. Unfortunately, debt snowballs in the wrong direction.

Going into debt to fund consumption is a terribly expensive mistake. Borrowing to consume more than you produce is the exact opposite of limiting consumption in order to invest. Investing means having a little less now to have a lot more later. Borrowing to consume means having a lot less later to have a little more now—not a good deal.

If you are growing consumer debt you are "negative investing" and all the power of compounding is working against you. I'm talking about using credit cards or other forms of debt to buy things like food, clothes, or entertainment that don't give a long-term return. Stop the negative spiral of consumer debt as soon as possible. Increase your productivity. Limit your consumption. Paying off high-interest debt may be a better investment than any other opportunity you have. Start there.

If you want specific guidance on managing personal finances and getting out of debt, access resources like MyMoney.gov or author Dave Ramsey's training materials. The steps to getting debt under control aren't complicated or hard to understand. It comes down to spending less than you earn. Easy to understand, but maybe hard to do.

Use Debt Selectively and Cautiously

A lot of people get in trouble with debt. In response to this, some financial authors recommend becoming totally debt free. If you want one simple rule about debt, that recommendation will not steer you too far wrong. The costs (missed opportunities) of using too little debt are far smaller than the costs of using too much debt.

At the same time, debt is useful and helpful in some circumstances. For some endeavors, borrowing money is essential.

Sometimes it makes sense to borrow money to own and use an asset that provides a return and has lasting value.

For example, the owner of a construction business might borrow money to purchase a backhoe. The backhoe has lasting value, and owning it provides a big return in construction productivity and savings versus renting one. The amount of the loan to purchase the backhoe would be less than the value of the backhoe. If the business has an $80,000 loan on a $100,000 backhoe, the business in effect owns 20% of a backhoe. The loan is secured by an asset, and the asset is not consumed faster than the loan is paid off. The productivity increase returned by the backhoe is much greater than the interest cost for the loan. This kind of debt can lead to a positive spiral of increased productivity and increased profits.

A couple of generations ago, a farmer near Mason City, Iowa, invested in a tractor at a time when all the other farmers were still using horses. They all thought he was crazy. The big increase in productivity powered his profits, and he reinvested those profits in buying more farmland. It wasn't long before he was farming more ground than anyone else around. Borrowing money to purchase highly productive assets like that tractor can make very good sense.

Similarly, a home mortgage is a loan secured by an asset, and the asset is not typically consumed faster than the loan is paid off. It's possible to come out ahead owning a home versus renting one, mortgage interest expense included. Home mortgage debt doesn't snowball in the wrong direction. It spreads out the cost of using your home over the time you use it.

Even if you have extra cash to pay down your mortgage, it may not be your best available return. As of this writing, home mortgage interest rates are, in effect, subsidized by the U.S. government through Federal Reserve bond buying, which makes them a very inexpensive form of debt. If you are generating an after-tax return on invested money greater than the after-tax rate of interest on your home mortgage, it may be rational to keep your mortgage. A return higher than your mortgage interest rate might be hard to find in the stock market, but it should be easy to find in your life, work, and business.

Borrowing at a low interest rate, and investing the borrowed money at a higher rate of return, is leverage. It has its place, and it has its hazards. In personal life and most small businesses, I recommend using it sparingly if at all. Large companies and asset-heavy businesses can and should make strategic use of debt to increase returns on equity. I'm not against leverage, within cautious and reasonable limits. Too much leverage is a lot of fun, until it isn't.

Overuse of debt will hurt you much more than underuse of debt. Use with caution.

Action Points

▸ If you haven't already, start investing your resources ASAP to maximize time for compounding growth to work.

▸ Limit your consumption and reinvest your profits even as investment returns start to roll in. Roll those profits into the snowball of compounding growth.

▸ Allocate your resources to your best-returning investment opportunities. A slightly higher ROI makes a big difference over many years of compounding.

▸ When your resources are small, your best-returning investment opportunities may be small opportunities in your personal life and work, not investments in large public markets.

▸ As your resources grow, expect to expand your search to larger investment opportunities that fit the amount of capital you need to reinvest.

▸ Look for opportunities for compounding growth of non-financial resources, too.

▸ Avoid compounding backward by borrowing money to increase consumption.

▸ Use debt selectively and cautiously to obtain productive assets or prudently leverage investment returns.

Engage Online

See how other readers want to "keep rolling the snowball" and add your thoughts at *www.aardsma.com/investingbook*.

13 >   Come Out Ahead Trading Your Time

In my early 20s I was employed. I traded 40 hours of my time each week for a modest wage. I earned enough at that job to support my family and pay my bills, and I'm grateful for that. Though I didn't know it, I was trading my time for much less than it was worth. I wasn't putting my available time resource on my best available return—not even close. And I wasn't delegating at all. My employer was delegating to me.

Then I started freelancing as a software developer. The clients who hired me to write software paid well. I was still trading my time for money, at a much higher hourly wage. Even at that higher return, I still wasn't putting my available time resource on my best available return.

Then I pivoted from selling my time as a freelancer, to spending my time building salable software products. For the first time I was investing my time in something that could earn a return far larger than any hourly wage. No longer was I the product. I was selling a product that was separate from me. This freed me of a time limitation, and set me up to begin delegating.

I hired a smart and reliable technician to perform software installs. He was not a software developer, so his hourly wage was far lower than what I could earn freelancing. For the first time, I was a *buyer* of time. I was trading my time for a high value, and buying time at a much lower price. I was coming out ahead on my time trades. I was beginning to break through the limitations of my own time.

This arrangement was not necessarily at the expense of my employee. If trading his time for that paycheck was his best available return on time, we could both come out ahead. As a high-potential person, he learned a lot on and off the job, and after a few years he became a full-time entrepreneur running his own business. Working for me wasn't his best available return on time for long. Like me, he moved up in the time-trading process.

When we started ATS Acoustics, I became a buyer of time on a bigger scale. We hired manufacturing workers and office workers. Soon the total time going into the business was 10, then 20 times what I could put in on my own. I was breaking free of my time limitations in a bigger way. And at the same time those workers were trading their time for a better return than they were earning before they came to work for ATS.

A couple of years later we started ATS Rentals, and the trend continued. I was a buyer of more than 40,000 hours of worker time every year. I was also deploying capital, earning a return on that, too. I spent most of my time leading, building businesses I owned, and investing in my own growth and development. I was earning very high returns on my time. I was coming out much further ahead on my time trades than I had been a few years before.

Then I ran into a problem: Though I had delegated a great deal, and I was earning a high financial return on my time, I had built businesses that weren't equipped to run without my daily presence. Areas like marketing strategy, difficult HR issues, and IT engineering still depended on me. I got stuck inside my own business creations.

If my vision for my life was simply to get rich, I could have stayed and continued investing my time building those profitable organizations. But there was more I wanted. I wanted to continue creating new things,

I wanted more face time with people, and I wanted to pay forward the gifts of leadership development and successful entrepreneurship.

I hadn't prepared those organizations to run without me. Honestly, I didn't have the gut-level optimism to believe they would grow into something much bigger. I don't feel confident those businesses would succeed long enough to need a second generation of leadership. I was focused on overcoming the challenges of that month or year. My vision and my confidence were too small. As a result, I fell behind the curve on preparing for a new level of time trading and delegation.

So I worked a day job as the leader of my businesses for a few years. During this time my managers continued to grow and develop. In early 2014, I took the leap, stepping away from daily management of those businesses. I put the responsibility in the hands of my managers, increasing their roles as leaders. I didn't know what would happen. I'd never delegated at that level before. I was prepared to make less money if that was the price of having free use of my time.

A year later, overall business results are better than ever. The leaders who replaced me have done an excellent job. I'm receiving more financial return with much less time investment than before. My managers and I are all coming out ahead on this change. The only losers are our business competitors, and I'm okay with that. I should have prepared to step away sooner, because running those businesses was not the best time trade I had available to me.

Now I have freedom to trade my time in pursuit of the life legacy I want to leave. I still spend some time doing things to earn money. I look for opportunities that give me the best available return for my time. And I look for opportunities that return things money can't buy, like impact on people and positive change in our world.

This story of my time trades (so far) ends very differently than it begins. Effective trades at the beginning led to increased returns, and options for even better time trades. It's a progression that I hope to continue, and I hope you will experience a similar progression.

Invest in Skills to Increase Returns on Your Time Trades

If you don't already have significant capital to invest, what you do with your time in the next decade will have a lot more impact on your future than what you do with your financial investments in the next decade.

You can't make an investment that will increase your lifespan, but you can make investments that increase the value of all your future time. Investing time (and maybe money) in developing skills is an important way to do this.

The return on skill development is greater when done earlier in life. You can put your new skills to use from the date you acquire them to the date you die. The longer that span is, the greater the payoff will be. We've got it right front-loading education at the beginning of our lives. So don't wait. Today is better than tomorrow when it comes to investing in your skills.

Formal education is one way to develop your skills, but it's hardly the only way, and not the highest-ROI way for many circumstances. Some professions such as medical and legal fields require specific education in order to qualify for a license to practice. If what you want to do requires convincing someone who values credentials to pick you, earning those credentials may be worthwhile. However, if what you want to do depends more on innovation, initiative, leadership, legwork, or the merits of the work itself, you may be better off proceeding to do it than spending years learning about it in a classroom.

I've observed people who want to start something or do some impactful work turn to education instead of starting. The fear of failure or not being good enough, or the simple fear of committing to go forward, finds a nice relief in the expensive, time-consuming, and sometimes unnecessary path of getting education first. As a two-time college dropout, I'll admit I'm biased on this one. You decide what is likely to be most effective for what you want to do.

Though I have my reservations about formal education, I am an unrestrained fan of learning. Learning in some fields is much more fun, effective, and efficient outside of the classroom. The Internet offers free access to more learning resources than you could ever consume. Because the marginal cost of sharing information on the Internet is approximately zero, the economics of free learning work. If you are a self-motivated independent learner, you can get the information and demonstrations you need for new skill development from sites like You-Tube, Khan Academy, and Wikipedia—all for free.

Combined with the right information, hands-on learning can be quite efficient and effective for many types of skills. Trial and error, test runs, and small-scale experiments are fantastic learning tools. Learning by doing also has the advantage of generating productive output and/or earning a wage while learning, in many cases.

I once spent some time between conference sessions with indie musician Hannah Elizabeth Smith. The night before, she had thrilled the crowd with her masterful main stage performance. While we chatted she was messing around on her guitar with skills so impressive and seemingly easy for her, I just had to shake my head and laugh.

In his book *Outliers*, Malcolm Gladwell describes the concept of 10,000 hours of practice to master anything, I asked 20-year-old Hannah if she thinks she has 10,000 hours of guitar practice in. After some quick mental math she said, "I think it's a lot more than that."

Calling her gifted would be an insult. She's spent a big fraction of the waking hours *in her life* practicing guitar. That's earned, not given.

Skill comes from practice. Skill is not handed out to a privileged few at birth. It's developed through investment of time in practice. That means no matter who you are, you can develop skills that raise the value of your time. This is an important way to power the positive spiral of compound investing, even when you have little to no money to invest.

Investment advantages come from the will or ability to do things others find difficult or impossible. Possessing a high level of skill is one way to get that. You can develop that kind of skill and use it as an investment advantage to earn a higher return on your time.

Skill is Different From Understanding

In Chapter 10 I talked about the investment advantage of thorough understanding. Thorough understanding of how something works gives you an advantage in making investment decisions about it. Skill is different. A high level of skill at something gives you an advantage in spending your time actually doing that thing.

I am reminded of this difference every time I practice flying airplanes. I understand the physics pretty well. Lift, inertia, aerodynamics, and engine function all make sense to me. Based on that understanding I can make informed decisions about how an airplane should be flown. This analytical understanding is almost no help with actually flying an airplane myself. A person with understanding knows why the airplane yaws when a crosswind hits. A pilot with skill pushes the right amount of rudder correction at the right time to stabilize the airplane. I'm still practicing that skill.

Understanding what technology is required for a startup company to succeed is one thing. Possessing the skill to create that technology in a lab is another. The first enables investment decisions. The second enables trading time for a high return. Both are useful. When you don't have much capital to make investment decisions, deciding to invest your time in increasing your skills might be a very good move.

Use Your Best Skills; Delegate the Rest

It's intuitive, of course, that you'll have an advantage working in a career that uses your best skills. If you are trained as a civil engineer, working as a retail cashier, for example, is probably not your best time investment opportunity. Others will be better than you are at cashiering, and you'll be better than they are at engineering. You'll likely seek a career that provides opportunity to put your best skills to use.

For most of my adult life my best skill was software development. When I started in my basement, long on time and short on cash, it was a no-brainer to invest my time in a business activity that used my software development skills. That's where I had an advantage that allowed me to earn a higher return on my time.

As I went forward into other businesses, my software skills continued to provide an advantage. I functioned as my own IT department for each of my startups, saving precious capital at early stages. I got into businesses that used a lot of software for logistics and digital marketing, and earned a high return on the time I spent creating that software.

After spending 10 years as a CEO, business leadership is now one of my best skills. I continue to look for opportunities to earn a high return on my time by putting my business leadership skills to use.

In economic terms, the rule is "Always export your comparative advantage." What you trade to others should be the thing you are best at producing, relative to everything else you could produce. Invest your time where you'll get the best return, and delegate the rest to others.

This applies to more than profit-making. If you are working on a nonprofit cause, it still makes sense for you to spend your time and energy on the parts you are better at compared to others, and let them do the parts they are better at compared to you.

Say it takes you one hour longer to change the oil in your car yourself than to have someone else do it. Say you can get paid $40 per hour using some other specialized skill in a freelance role. $40 per hour is the opportunity cost of your time. And say your local shop can change the oil in your car for $20 in labor. You can "buy" that hour of time from the shop for only $20, and "sell" it for $40. You come out $20 ahead if you take your car to the oil change store, and $20 *behind* if you change that oil yourself.

Paying someone to do what you could do yourself may conflict with ingrained values of frugality and self-sufficiency. The thing is, it's not truly frugal to spend $40 of time to save $20 of cash. Make sure you come out ahead on your time trades. *Delegate everything you can delegate for less than the cost of your time.*

If the current value of your time is $10 per hour instead of $40 per hour, this decision changes. Now you come out $10 ahead if you change the oil yourself, and $10 behind if you take it to the store. This illustrates the power of increasing the value of your time. As you increase the value you can trade your time for, you open up more and more opportunity to delegate *and come out ahead*. This maximizes the use of your most precious resource, your time.

><

A consultant who gets paid $1,000 an hour can and should delegate just about everything, and focus her time on the consulting itself, the part that nobody but she can do. She should have an assistant answering the phone, checking the mail, booking her travel, scheduling her meetings, processing the client contracts, and so on. Economically speaking, she should not be mowing her own lawn, spending more than a few minutes to search for the best deal on a new car, or even spending time driving herself places. Anything that costs (or saves) less than $1,000 per hour of her time should be delegated to someone else. She'd come out $980 behind if she changed her own oil. Frugal with money, in some sense, yes. Good investment, absolutely not.

Often this type of delegation decision requires comparing a non-monetary value to a monetary one. This goes back to knowing what you really want. For example, I could hire a nanny to raise my kids for less than the value of my time, but the non-monetary value of the relationship with my kids is worth more to me than the money I could generate with my time elsewhere. I don't feel the same way about spending time with my car while changing the oil.

When Passion Doesn't Pay Well

Some people find themselves in a situation where their best marketable skill doesn't align with their passion and what's really important to them. For example, a successful lawyer with high earning potential may find he has no passion for the practice of law. A simple economic perspective says he should use his best skill and delegate the rest. That means to spend a lot of time practicing law, and pay others to do most other things. This is the right prescription if the future he wants is maximum wealth regardless of quality of life.

Back in Chapter 1 we talked about the importance of reflecting before you race. Your "best return" is the return that contributes the most to the long-term future you desire. If our lawyer is passionate about justice for victims of human trafficking and wants to leave a legacy of positive impact in that area, he might choose to leave his high-paying corporate law job and go work for a legal justice nonprofit in Africa. The return in terms of dollars would be lower. The return in terms of bringing about the future he wants might be much higher.

It's a wonderful thing when passion, purpose, and lucrative financial returns all line up around one activity. It's much easier to stay inspired when your activities are in line with your future vision. I feel beyond grateful that entrepreneurship has been that way for me. Sometimes that combination is available all in one package. Sometimes it's not. When your passion and your best economic return lead in different directions, you'll have to answer tough questions about what kind of future you really want.

How important is economic success to you? What are you willing to give up to get more of what you love? Is the work you're doing to pay the bills helping you move toward what you love, or is it actually holding back?

If you are doing something you don't really want to do because it pays well, either use that money for what you do truly value, or line up your life with the future you really want by changing what you're doing with your time. If it's hard, but it's your best way to move toward the future you really want, do the hard thing. If it's not moving you toward the future you really want, stop doing it. Line up your actions with your intended future.

Am I suggesting the passionate artist quit her job and go full time doing the street art she loves so much? Probably not, unless a life as a starving artist is the future she really wants. It's quite possible that job she lacks passion for is a key part of making the future she really wants—a future that includes food, shelter, and a way to fund her art. Look realistically at the whole future picture. Don't base your decisions on a fantasy that isn't backed by a workable plan. I'd advise that artist to build a foundation for doing more of what she loves by looking for art-related employment, or building a fan base, for example, and to keep her day job until that foundation is in place.

On the other hand, sometimes making a big change to engage fully in your passion isn't a fantasy-driven leap, it's a brave and realistic path to the future you really want. A second-generation business owner "stuck" in the family business, for example, may have very realistic prospects in another field he is more passionate about, but find it difficult for a number of reasons to make the switch.

To make the pursuit of your passion work you'll need to possess or develop the abilities and other resources that enable success in that area. You'll also need to outline a realistic plan for doing what you love, paying bills, and maintaining the other parts of life that matter to you.

The choice to leave your status quo and engage in what you love should be based on realistic projections of the future, as best as you can see. Don't leap based on a fantasy, and don't stay put because of fear.

How to Delegate Well

It's in your interest to delegate when others can do tasks at a lower cost than the value of the time it would take you to do those tasks. At the same time, there are hazards in trusting others to do tasks that matter to you. Here are a few thoughts on delegating well.

Give responsibility to qualified people. Whether you trust a teenager to mow your lawn, a contractor to build your real estate, an employee to serve customers, or a corporation to manufacture your supplies, it matters whom you select. The more that's at stake, the more due diligence you'll need to invest to ensure the provider you select is competent to perform the way you want them to. Those who lack the required competencies cannot be trusted to deliver, no matter how good their intentions.

Give responsibility to motivated people. People respond to incentives, and people respond to their engrained character. Make sure both are pointing toward the behavior you want from the people and providers you select.

If you want your managers to increase profits, their pay should probably increase when your profits increase. If you want your assembly workers to care about quality, their pay should probably not be based solely on speed. Job security, praise, and opportunity to advance should flow to those who do the work and treat people the way you want them to.

If you want employees to treat customers with respect and enthusiasm, give that responsibility to people who've had those behaviors engrained in them since they were toddlers. Select people whose internal compass is aligned with the results you want.

Communicate clear expectations. Whether you are hiring a person or a company, they need to know what outcomes you expect, what you count as success, and what is not acceptable. It's your job to be clear. Compared to a solo project, it takes extra time and extra communication skills to ensure this clarity. You can read your own mind. Nobody else can.

Let go, gradually. Delegation is a process of increasing responsibility and increasing autonomy over time. In most cases it's not a good idea to pick someone, turn them loose, and walk away. Delegation of high-level responsibility is usually a multi-year process. As trust and skills are built, and you've instilled the values and behaviors you want, you can let go more and more. At the same time, don't hang on too much or too long. Nobody likes to be micromanaged. Find an appropriate pace to transition responsibility.

As Time and Money Investments Pay Off, Reinvest the Extra Time and Money

As you increase the value of your time, and maximize your return by doing more of what you are best at, and less of what you aren't, your returns will increase. You'll have more time and money available.

"Reinvest your returns" applies here, too. Invest that extra time to create long-term value. Develop even more skills. Build your personal character. Deepen your network of relationships. Work overtime. Run a side business. Take on a freelance job. Build something.

Owning your own business can be an especially advantageous way to put your time to optimally productive use. The flexibility to get increased returns by investing increased time and the built-in opportunity to delegate to employees are both fantastic benefits to the owner.

Skill development and higher wage earnings are not sufficient to keep this positive spiral growing beyond the limits of your time. Increasing the value of your time helps increase your returns and generate excess resources, but it doesn't scale beyond 24 hours in a day and about 100 years in a lifetime.

To break beyond that scale, you'll need to invest part of the proceeds from your time trades in things that can grow without requiring proportionately more time input from you. As we've discussed before, building a business is one way to do that.

The same concepts can apply to not-for-profit endeavors. Building a movement that incorporates the time of many volunteers and/or employees enables the returns (measured in impact or positive change) to scale far beyond with the visionary founder could do alone.

Like owning stock, other financial investments also scale without requiring more time inputs. Making a decision about a $10 billion bond purchase doesn't necessarily take more time than making a decision about a $1,000 bond purchase. Capital investments scale in the context of some very, very large markets.

Trade Your Time Well

If you desire a bigger future, don't trade all your productive time for money and spend all that money in lifestyle consumption. This is like treading water. You get to stay alive, and that's about it.

You can intentionally invest your time to increase the value of your time, like learning a new marketable skill. You can intentionally invest your time to build something of long-term value, like a product, a relationship, or a reputation. You can trade your time for the maximum wage available to you, and invest that money on your best available return. You can spend some of that money to delegate lower-paying tasks to others, and put your freed-up time to productive use. You can invest the proceeds of all these constructive activities in opportunities that scale beyond the limitations of your own time.

You can't buy time and add it to your lifespan, but you can trade money to other people in exchange for their time. This can free up your time, and even more importantly, enable projects that require many times more person-hours of time than you alone could spend on those projects in a lifetime.

As your productivity and investment returns increase, trading your money for other people's time becomes a much better deal than trading your time for other people's money.

Paradoxically, unless you inherit wealth, the only way you can access this better deal starts by spending your time to get money. Here's the sequence. Be productive with your time. Limit consumption. Invest the extra. Use the extra money that creates to free up your time. Reinvest your time at a higher level of productivity. Repeat.

Repeat that long enough, and your investments will be producing so much return that almost all of your time will be yours to do with as you please. You will no longer have to spend your time to get money, because you won't need the money. You'll invest your time in the future and the legacy you want.

Action Points

▸ Invest time and maybe money in developing skills that increase your returns on future time investments.

▸ Allocate your available time to where you will receive the best available return. Do a lot of what you're best at.

▸ Define your best return in terms of the long-term future you really want.

▸ Delegate all kinds of tasks that others can do for less cost to you than the value of the time it would take you to do those tasks.

▸ Carefully select qualified and motivated people and providers to delegate to, and give responsibility at an appropriate pace, over time.

▸ As these steps increase the time and money you have available, reinvest those surpluses in even more skill development and even more delegation, to keep the positive spiral going.

▸ As your resources grow, invest in opportunities that can scale unconstrained by your time limitations.

Engage Online

Take a quiz on how you currently trade your time and how you might trade it differently at *www.aardsma.com/investingbook*.

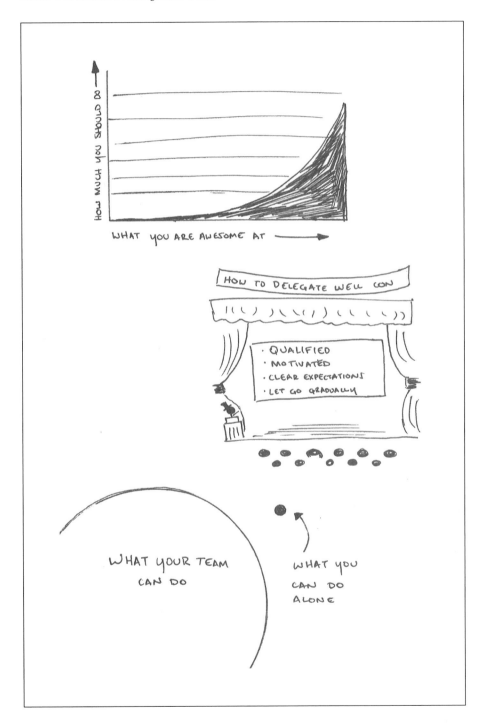

14 >   Bet Big on Your Big Adventures

Long before I knew him, my friend and mentor Greg Campbell was a hardworking executive for Sears, Roebuck & Company. In the 1980s he worked his way up in real estate–related management positions within Sears. At the time, Sears was into a lot of businesses beyond retailing. Coldwell Banker Real Estate, Allstate Insurance, and Discover Card, for example, were part of Sears.

About 1990, Coldwell Banker was a billion-dollar business that was losing a lot of money. The leadership of Sears asked Greg to take on the role of executive vice president of Coldwell Banker. He accepted, and took on the huge responsibility of running the entire business.

Greg is a disciplined and intentional leader, and that was just what Coldwell Banker needed. In just a few years he led changes in structure and business practices that brought the company from big losses to breaking even. Greg was confident that profitability would soon follow.

Then the top management at Sears came under pressure to get out of the non-retail businesses they were diversified into. Sears decided to put Coldwell Banker up for sale.

Greg had a big advantage in this big opportunity: Not only did he have a front-row seat to the inner workings of Coldwell Banker, and the trend toward profitability, he was at the helm leading that change. He thoroughly understood the change, and he was directing it. That was a big advantage.

Greg saw this big opportunity and this big advantage, and he bet big on it. He cooperated with a group of investors to buy Coldwell Banker from Sears. He became an owner of what he was building. He told me he put "every dime he had" into that investment. He didn't diversify. He concentrated, to the extreme.

Greg and the investment group intended to own the business long term and run it as a profitable enterprise. Greg's leadership did result in profitability. Then, unexpectedly, a larger group offered a high price to purchase Coldwell Banker. Greg and the other current owners decided it was just too high a price to pass up, changed their plans, and sold at a big gain. The ROI on that concentrated investment was off the charts.

Since then Greg has been able to focus decades of his time on what matters most to him, including mentoring young leaders like me, and providing significant financial and relational support to not-for-profit causes he believes in.

Concentrate Your Investment on Your Best Return, if You Can

Diversification is spreading out your resources, and your risk, across multiple investments. Concentration is the opposite: putting a lot of eggs in one basket.

Diversification is a valuable tool for protecting your overall resources from being severely reduced by bad luck or bad decisions related to one investment. The average return from a group of 10 or 30 or 100 separate investments is much more predictable than the return from a single investment.

Diversification is what makes insurance companies work. It's impossible to predict whether or not I will get into a car accident on any given day. But it's easy to predict with reasonable accuracy what percentage of one million car insurance customers will get into an accident on any given day. I figure it's about 0.015%. Additionally, if I wreck 100% of the car I drive on a given day, that's a much more negative event for me than for my insurer to receive claims for accidents on perhaps 0.015% of the cars they insure on a given day. Diversification of risk across a large group makes the results smoother and more predictable.

This diversification makes sense because—*and only because*—the insurance company does not know which drivers will have an accident claim at any given time. When a customer has a claim, the insurance company takes perhaps a 2,000% loss on that year's premium. When a customer does not have a claim, the insurance company receives around a 75% profit on that year's premium. If the insurance company specifically knew who would have an accident and who would not have an accident, they would accept only future-accident-free drivers and make huge profits. Furthermore, they would not need to diversify. Even insuring just one future-accident-free driver would be an acceptable risk and a reasonable guarantee of profitable results.

Diversification actually *reduces* the insurance company's profits versus the theoretical scenario of knowing the future returns on each driver they insure. Nonetheless, because individual future accidents cannot be specifically predicted, insurance companies have no choice but to diversify the risk across a large group, where they can predict the results in aggregate.

As investors, we can take some lessons from this.

Diversification is a useful tool when you can't predict the returns of individual investments. The more ability you have to predict which investments will give the best returns, the more it makes sense to concentrate your resources there. This concentration is another way to say the principle we've looked at all throughout this book. Take your available resources and use them on the investment opportunities that will give the best return.

Greg concentrated all of his financial resources to buy part of Coldwell Banker because he had the information to be quite confident that it offered his best available return, by far. What he did took courage, and it involved risk. The story could have ended much differently. But Greg felt that risk was acceptable, and he went all in. With such a big advantage on such a big opportunity, he concentrated. He didn't diversify.

When I started my basement software business, I concentrated nearly all my work time on it. It was my best return by far, and the risks of loss were minimal, so it made sense to do that.

When I started ATS Acoustics, I concentrated nearly all of my financial net worth in that business. For years after that I continued to reinvest nearly all of my profits into that business. When I started ATS Rentals, I poured a lot of capital into it, too. This kept my resources concentrated in the businesses I owned. I estimate that 95% of all my financial resources were devoted to ATS Acoustics, and later to ATS Rentals, even six to seven years after I started. I was all in on my own companies.

Sometimes I got heartburn about this. I knew I was taking very concentrated risk. A lawsuit, a product safety issue, or any number of other calamities I pondered could have brought the thing down. I also knew I had huge advantages in this businesses and a strong likelihood of generating higher ROI than I could reliably find anywhere else.

We did set aside a little for retirement each quarter. My wife and I were young, so the amount we needed to save for our old age was pretty small. Thank you, compound growth.

Other than that little diversification, I was all in. This wasn't because the businesses were mine, and I wanted to invest in myself. It's because the ROI was high and the risks were small by comparison. If I had diversified my investments at that time, it would have cost me a great deal in missed opportunity.

Bet big on your big advantages.

Diversify When You Need To

Diversification reduces the chance of huge losses, and it also reduces the chance of huge gains. Diversification violates the rule of investing your resources on the best available return. However, when you are unable or unwilling to accept the risk of huge losses, you have no choice but to diversify your investments and accept returns that are closer to average.

Diversification has another downside. Your workload as an investor is increased when you diversify and seek superior returns. Now instead of finding one superior opportunity, you need to find three, or five, or 10. That's harder.

Nonetheless, it's rarely smart to bet the farm on one thing, so often we need to do that extra work to keep our risk exposure to acceptable levels. For this reason, don't do something like put your entire net worth on one stock. That's too much trust in a management team you don't know, making decisions you can't override, in a business you can only observe from a distance.

Allocate a lot of resources to your best opportunities, and at the same time ensure that in a downside scenario you'll have enough resources to live to play another day. Greg still had highly marketable executive experience. I had software skills and a little retirement account to fall back on. Neither of us would have gone hungry or homeless if our big bets failed.

For individuals this might mean keeping an emergency fund of a few months' income in a safe, low-returning savings account. It's not your best return, but it significantly reduces the risk of poor decisions and long-term negative outcomes from unfortunate disruptions like a job loss or an illness. It also means spreading out your resources across multiple investments, even if one of them appears to be better than the others, to reduce the risk of a devastating loss.

Diversify When You Have No Advantage

If you have a reliable and time-efficient way to predict returns on individual stocks, it's rational to concentrate your investments on a few of them (perhaps 10 different stock investments). Most investors have no such advantage, meaning their expected return from the stock(s) they pick is the same as the average stock market overall. Diversification offers the same expected return, with much less risk of an unlucky bad result.

Broad stock index funds offer a remarkably cheap and easy way to diversify. It's buying a share of a fund that buys one of everything, so to speak. If you have capital that's not better used elsewhere and you have no advantage at picking stocks, index funds are probably the way to go. This type of no-selection advantage, one-of-everything diversification also brings the significant advantage of requiring no investment of time attempting to pick the winners.

It also avoids paying someone else an investment management fee to attempt to pick the winners for you. Most investment managers don't have an advantage at picking stocks, either. And most of us have no way to tell the future winning managers from the future average ones. Lacking any advantage here, index funds make sense for most of us.

Remember, though, to look globally at all your resources and all your opportunities. It may be that some skills training, or an employee hire, or starting a business, or spending money to reduce your long-term lifestyle expenses would be a much better investment opportunity for you than a stock index fund.

I view diversified public market investments as useful to me in two scenarios. First, they function well as a low-risk long-term backup fund in case of total disaster in my concentrated endeavors. Second, they provide a readily available last resort when I have resources to invest at a time when I can't find an opportunity where I have an advantage.

Many people who are not involved in business, or dedicated to investment activities of one kind or another, may not have opportunities to invest significant amounts of money where they have an advantage. This makes diversified index funds useful to a large number of people.

Concentration is Not Just for Financial Investments

If you are investing time as a volunteer, or investing time building relationships, or investing your skills in a project, it probably makes sense to concentrate more than diversify.

When you know which cause, which organization, which relationships will best align with the future you desire, it probably makes sense to concentrate your efforts there. Advocating for 10 good causes is not likely to be as effective as advocating more thoroughly for one or two. If you know the specific place you can make the biggest difference, it will reduce, not increase, your total impact if you spread out your efforts to include work in other places. There's power in laser-like focus over an extended period of time.

The same is likely true when you are investing money to make a difference, instead of to make more money for yourself. For example, donating to one or a few causes in which you have advantages such as understanding, connections, or relationships is likely to make more difference than diversifying your investment across a large number of organizations.

Raise Your Eyes

As we come to the end of this book, I want to ask you to act on what you've read. Sometimes moving from ideas to actions gets really scary, especially when you set out to create a future that deeply matters. Taking action requires courage in the face of fear. It's uncomfortable, and it's worth it.

For my first 30 years of life I focused most of my energy on getting by. I kept my head down and worked hard on my own challenges. I assumed most people were okay, and I was the only one finding life to be such a difficult journey.

As a side effect of my struggle, I worked hard to build a lot of things, and I experienced a lot of success. I also reached out for much-needed help, and experienced great relationships with employees, friends, and mentors. Those built into me.

Eventually I took a breath and looked around. I raised my eyes to meet the gaze of the people walking by me. I noticed they were struggling, too. As absurd as it seemed at first, I began to realize that I could help—that in various ways I could be generous and have an impact, as others had with me.

As I engaged with all kinds of people in this world full of humanity, I saw that many people aspire to invest their time and money well. Some people noticed my investment results and wanted to learn about that from me. This book is my response. It's one result of my shift from head down to eyes raised.

I'd like to ask you to do the same. Raise your eyes. Look into the faces of those you share this earth with. See the struggles and the opportunities, and dare to believe that you can make a significant contribution.

The contributions you make might be wildly different than mine, and that's good. As a human race we face many challenges: political, economic, technological, and human. There is work worth doing. There are people worth serving. We all need each other to step up and start, to use our time and money resources to their fullest potential. That's how new solutions to old problems get discovered and implemented. That's how we keep our countries stable and prosperous, and create opportunities for those who follow behind us. That's how we live up to the full measure of the potential we are given.

It takes more than a generous heart to make a significant contribution. It takes clarity of vision and intentional action. It takes skillful investment of a broad range of resources. When we live and work with the kind of investment savvy we've talked about in this book, our resources grow and our influence increases.

Develop your advantages and put them to work making your life and our world better. Lean into the difficult work. Most importantly, start.

Nothing Happens Until You Start

It's not enough to have resources, even abundant resources. It's not enough to have advantages, even big ones. Brilliant ideas, bold visions, and masterful plans are worth nothing if you don't act on them. You must take the risk to bet big on your big advantages.

Your fear might be a little uneasy about you dreaming big, because God forbid that gets you excited enough to do something. But starting is risky in a way that dreaming is not. When you start declaring your intentions, making commitments, and taking action, your fear will hit every panic button it's got and stage a full-blown opposition. What you choose to do in that moment will make more difference to your future than maybe anything else.

Back in that creepy, unimpressive basement, on my first day of self-employment, there was a whole lot I didn't have and a whole lot I didn't know. I didn't have any credentials, much money, or many relationships. I didn't know I was taking the first step toward big success and unimagined opportunities. I had no way to know if it would even work out at all. None of that mattered, because I did the most important thing: I started.

You can start with the resources you have. You can start with the knowledge you have. You have enough vision of the future to take the next step. Don't tell yourself you'll start intentionally creating the future you want after you read more books, get more education, or get a little older. If you choose a safe and inactive detour, your fear will pat you on the shoulder and smile with relief. Action crisis averted. And opportunity lost.

Acting on what you know is the hard part, and the part that brings all the rewards for you and the people you impact. Don't miss your opportunities. Take the first action step. Nothing happens until you start.

I hope you intentionally invest your time, money, and all your resources to create the future you really want. That's investing with purpose.

Thank you for listening, and for acting. I am grateful.

Invest well, my friend. Don't wait. Go.

Action Points

- If the level of risk is acceptable to you, concentrate your resources on the investments where you have the biggest advantages.

- Diversify when you need to reduce your risk of a large loss or below-average returns, knowing this will also reduce your chance of a large gain or above-average returns.

- Diversify when you have no advantage at picking the winners, and the cost of diversification is worth the risk-reduction it provides.

- When investing time, and when investing money for non-financial results, use the power of concentration to increase your returns.

- Don't waste time in a holding pattern rationalized by what you don't have. Start with what you have.

Engage Online

Share how you will start investing differently at *www.aardsma.com/investingbook*.

> Index <

Index

> About the Author <

Starting without wealth, connections, or anyone's permission, Mark Aardsma became the entrepreneur behind multiple successful businesses. Using what he had and building from the ground up, he led two of his companies to the multi-million-dollar level. One was featured three years in a row on *Inc.* magazine's list of fastest-growing companies.

Mark is an active CEO, a venture investor in early-stage companies, and a patient investor in financial markets. He also does coaching, speaking, and writing intended to encourage his audiences to face their fears and live and work the way they really want to. He lives with his wife and four children in Champaign, Illinois.